Unders... g the Human Body

The Heart, Lungs and Blood

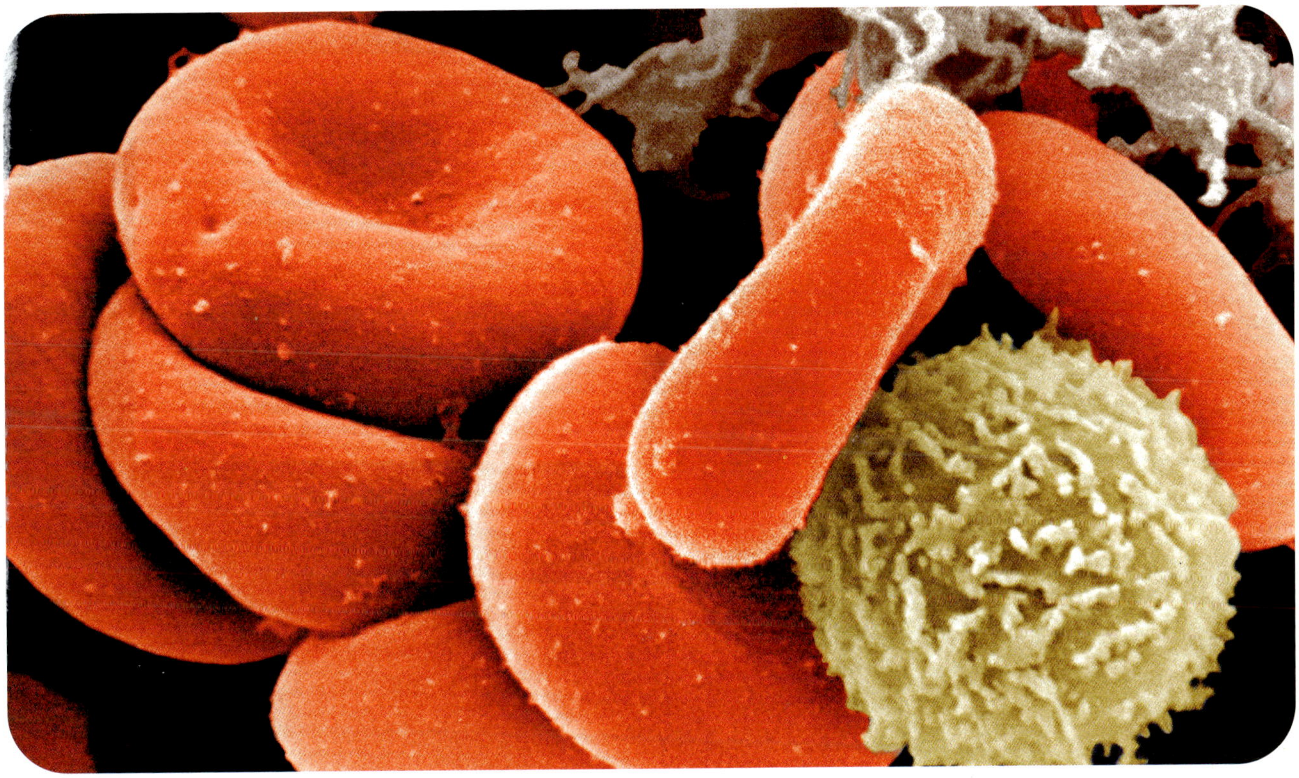

Sarah Levete

First published in 2009 by Wayland
338 Euston Road
London NW1 3BH

Wayland Australia
Level 17/207 Kent Street
Sydney NSW 2000

British Library Cataloguing in Publication Data
Levete, Sarah
The heart, lungs and blood. - (Understanding the human body)
1. Cardiovascular system - Juvenile literature
I. Title
612.1

ISBN: 978 0 7502 5727 5

Produced for Wayland by Discovery Books Limited
Managing Editor: Laura Durman
Editor: Kathryn Walker
Wayland editor: Katie Powell
Design and illustrations: sprout.uk.com
Picture research: Rachel Tisdale
Series consultant: Sue Hyem

Printed in China

Wayland is a division of Hachette Children's Books, an Hachette UK Company.
www. hachette.co.uk

Photo acknowledgements: Getty images: title page & p. 8 (Yrgos Nikas), p. 10 (Dr Kessel & Dr Kardon), p. 34 (Ralph Hutchings); Istockphoto.com: cover & p. 42 (Jared Cassidy), pp. 6, 9, 14 (Nikolay Suslov), p. 15 (David Lewis), p. 37 (Mikkel William Nielsen); Nasa: p. 13; Science Photo Library: p. 12 (Manfred Kage/Peter Arnold Inc.), p. 24 (BSIP VEM), p. 32 (Med Images); Shutterstock: p. 17 (Renaud Thomas), p. 19 (Yuri Arcurs), p. 21 (Evok20), p. 22 (Dario Sabljak), p. 23 (Laurence Gough), p. 26 (Supri Suharjoto), p. 27 (Marin), p. 31 (Specta), p. 33 (Zany Zeus), p. 36 (Morgan Lane Photography), p. 38 (Galina Barskaya), p. 39 (Simone van den Berg), p. 40 (Martin Kucera), p. 41 (Troy Casswell), p. 43 (Adam Radosavljevic)

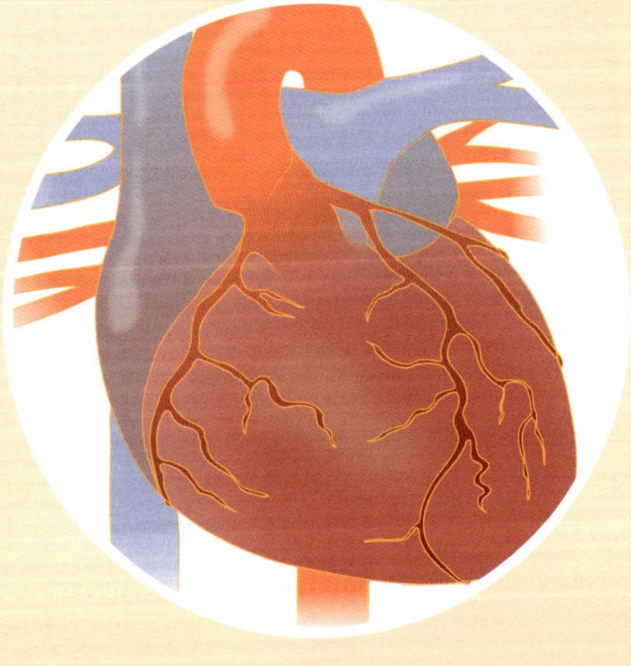

Contents

Breath, beat and flow

Every day, every minute, every second, your body is hard at work. Blood flows from head to toe, your heart beats and you breathe in and out. Without any conscious effort, your body works day and night. The heart, blood and lungs are central to this non-stop activity. The heartbeat, flow of blood and breath are all involuntary actions that are essential to life. In this book we investigate how the breath, blood and heart keep the body at work, rest and play.

The same, but different

No two human bodies are identical on the inside or the outside. But there are standard physical structures inside the human body. The patterns that these structures follow allow doctors and scientists to understand the healthy function and action of each organ. There are often small variations in each

Your body works 24 hours a day, seven days a week, relying constantly on the action of your heart, blood and lungs.

person's organs. These may be due to size, position or the effect of illnesses on a particular organ or system.

Body systems

A collection of organs working together to carry out specific tasks is known as a body system. The cardiovascular system is the workings of the heart ('cardio' means relating to the heart) and the blood ('vascular' means relating to the blood vessels). The respiratory system ('respire' means to breathe) is the workings of the lungs, nose and airways.

The cardiovascular system is a complex network of vessels and capillaries that carry blood around the body, pumped by the beating action of the heart. The transport of the blood is also called the circulatory system. The respiratory system provides oxygen for the body's cells and gets rid of carbon dioxide. The oxygen and carbon dioxide are carried in the blood.

Cells and tissue

Cells are tiny units in the human body that are invisible to the eye unless viewed under a microscope. There are over 50 billion cells in your body. Different types of cells are adapted to carry out different tasks. Groups of cells form tissues that make up the body's structures. Some tissues, such as the skin, are soft and others, such as fingernails, are hard. Blood is a liquid tissue, while organs, such as the heart and lungs, are made up of different types of tissues.

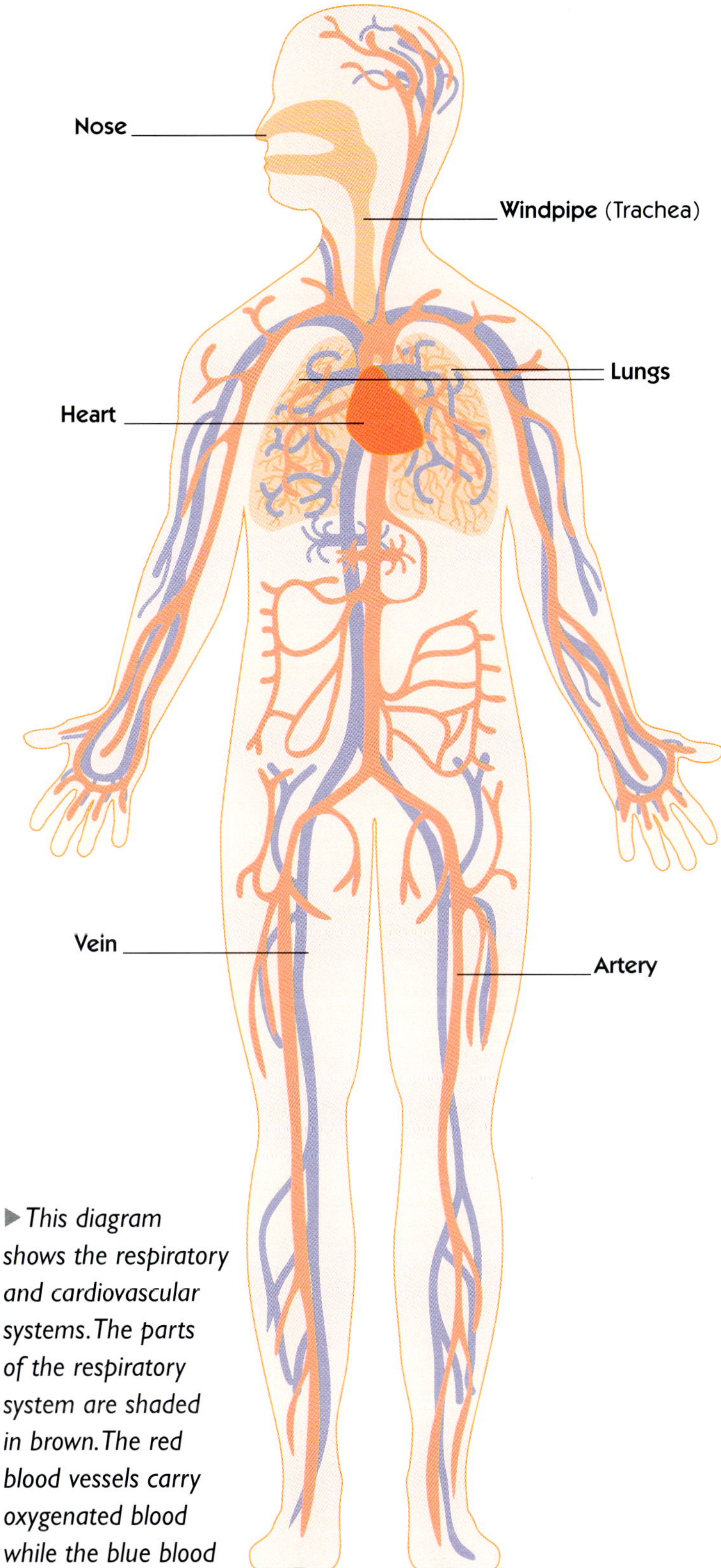

▶ *This diagram shows the respiratory and cardiovascular systems. The parts of the respiratory system are shaded in brown. The red blood vessels carry oxygenated blood while the blue blood vessels carry deoxygenated blood.*

Blood

Without blood, there is no life in the human body. You may only be aware of your blood when you cut yourself, but it is constantly rushing around inside you, keeping your body clean, fed and warm.

Blood composition

Blood looks red, but more than half of it is yellow. Over 50 per cent of blood is made up of a straw-coloured liquid called plasma. This is a mixture of water, proteins, mineral salts and glucose. The rest of the blood is composed of billions of cells called corpuscles, some red and some white, together with tiny cell fragments called platelets, or thrombocytes. Plasma transports the blood cells around the body, with red blood cells in the middle and white blood cells along the edge.

Body facts

There are between five and six litres (9 and 10.5 pints) of blood in the body of an average-sized male adult.

In a drop of blood the size of a pinhead, there are about 250 million red blood cells, 16 million platelets and 375,000 white blood cells!

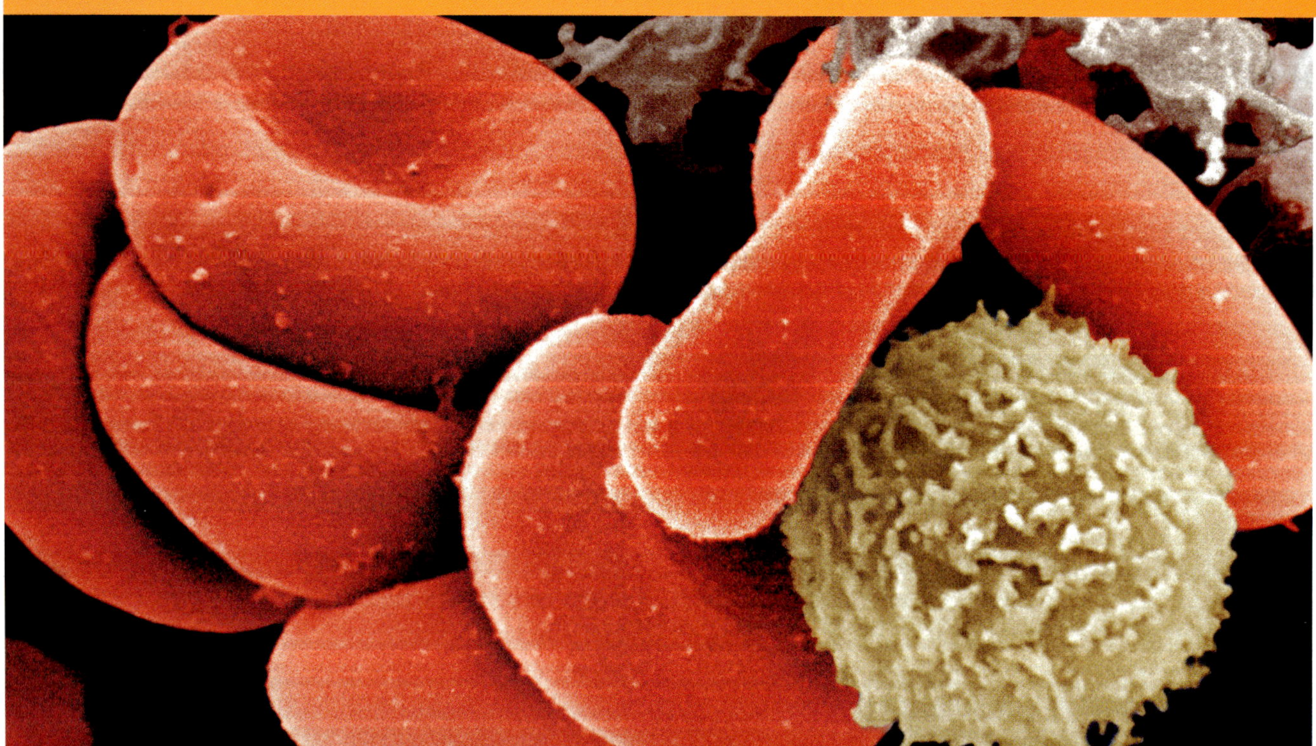

This photograph, taken with a microscope, shows red blood cells and one white blood cell (the pale object on the right). Red blood cells are doughnut–shaped but can change shape as they squash up to pass through tiny blood vessels.

Corpuscles and platelets

Red blood cells are also called erythrocytes. There are more of these in your body than any other cell. Red blood cells contain a chemical called haemoglobin. This is responsible for carrying oxygen in the blood and makes the blood look red.

White blood cells (also called leukocytes) are the body's defenders. They travel around the body fighting off the bacteria. Platelets are particles that are even smaller than red blood cells. They play an important part in forming blood clots to prevent blood loss.

Busy blood

Blood supplies cells with oxygen and nutrients. Nutrients are the tiny parts of food that the body needs to stay alive and keep healthy. Cells break down these nutrients in chemical reactions to produce energy. The health, growth and action of almost every part of the body depends upon the nutrients supplied in the blood.

Eating foods such as spinach and nuts helps maintain healthy levels of iron in the blood.

Investigate

Oxygen-carrying haemoglobin gives human blood its reddish colour. Some animals' blood is not red because they have other ways of carrying oxygen around the body. For instance, a lobster's blood is blue when it is oxygenated (rich in oxygen). Find out which other animals do not have red blood and why.

Anaemia

If there is not enough haemoglobin in the blood or there are not enough red blood cells, a person will lack energy and look pale. This condition is called anaemia. A mineral called iron is needed to form haemoglobin, so to cure anaemia a person can take iron pills. These will boost the number of red blood cells and the strength of haemoglobin. People with anaemia can also help themselves by eating foods that are rich in iron, such as spinach, red meat and nuts.

Blood on the move

Blood doesn't move around freely in the body – it travels along a carefully controlled one-way system. This system is made up of a complex network of tubes called blood vessels. Some vessels, such as arteries, are wide and thick. Others, such as capillaries, are thinner than a human hair. Laid out end to end, this transport system measures more than 100,000 kilometres (62,500 miles).

Arteries

Blood is pumped away from the heart into blood vessels called arteries. These tubes have strong walls that won't burst under the surge of blood that travels one metre (3 feet) every two seconds. The inner lining of an artery is smooth, allowing the blood to flow without any restrictions.

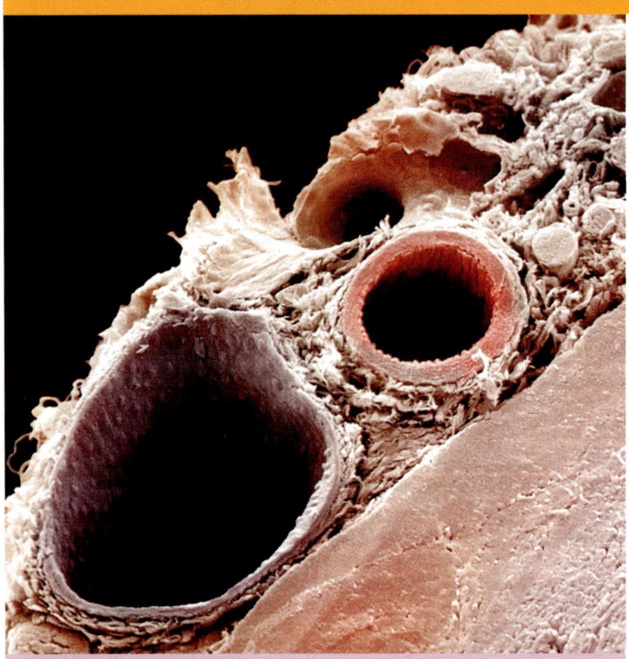

This photo shows a cross section of a vein (left) and an artery (right). The vein is wider than the artery, but its walls are thinner.

The arteries branch out and spread around the body, becoming thinner as they do so. They divide into smaller vessels called arterioles. The inner lining of an arteriole can contract or squeeze together and slow down the racing blood from the artery.

Arterioles lead into capillaries. Blood slows down as it travels along the capillaries – flowing at about 1 m (3 ft) every half hour.

Capillaries

There are thousands of capillaries everywhere in the body. These microscopic vessels are like an intricate web. They lie next to almost every cell in the body. Nutrients and oxygen in the blood's plasma easily pass across a capillary's paper-thin wall to reach the cell. Capillaries join up and lead into thicker veins.

Veins

When the blood has passed to the cells and delivered its nutrients, it continues its round-the-body trip, returning to the heart. Vessels called veins carry the returning blood. Look at your wrist and you may be able to see slightly raised or darker lines under your skin. These are your veins. They have valves, like stoppers, to prevent blood from flowing backwards.

Non-stop conveyor belt

All arteries except the pulmonary artery (see below) carry oxygenated blood away from the heart. This blood has received plenty of oxygen from the lungs. The arteries carry the oxygenated blood to the rest of the body.

By the time the capillaries have finished delivering this oxygen to different cells, the blood that then flows into the veins is low in oxygen, or deoxygenated. This deoxygenated blood journeys back to the heart to receive a new burst of oxygen. The newly oxygenated blood continues its delivery service around the rest of the body. It is like a non-stop conveyor belt.

Getting the oxygenated blood

One part of the cardiovascular system takes blood to and from the lungs. Blood travels from the heart to the lungs in the pulmonary artery. This blood is deoxygenated because its oxygen has been delivered to the body tissues. After it has collected oxygen from the lungs, the blood returns to the heart via the pulmonary vein. There it is sent to the rest of the body via the other arteries.

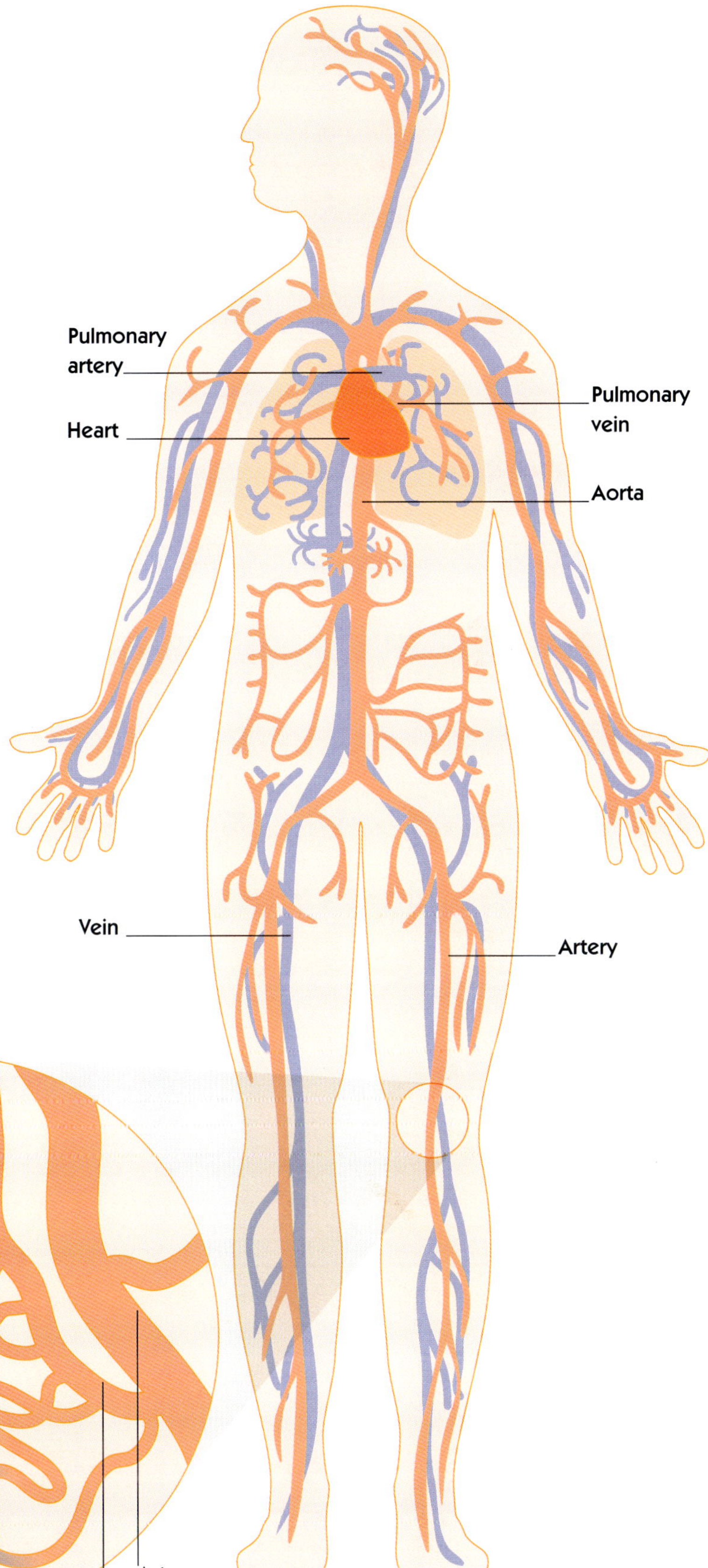

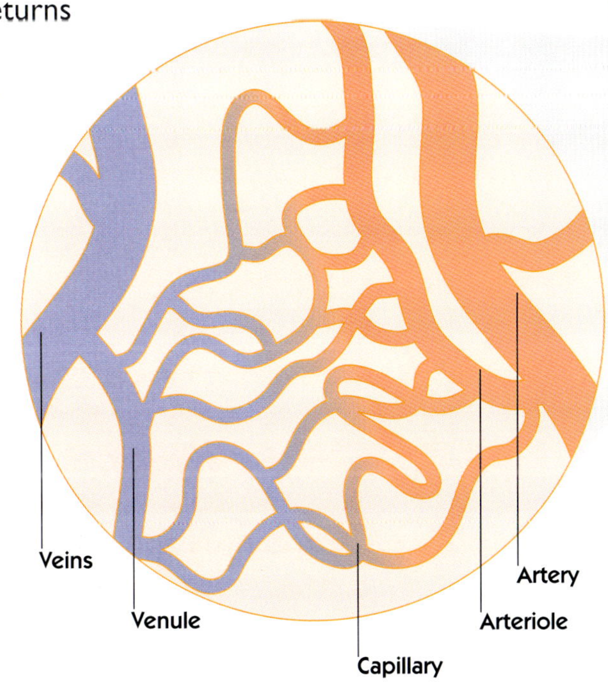

▶ *The aorta is the largest artery in the body. It branches into other arteries, arterioles and thin capillaries. Blood from capillaries is collected in venules which branch out into larger veins.*

Blood protection

White blood cells are like the body's soldiers. They help to fight off infection and enemy invaders, destroying germs such as disease-carrying bacteria and viruses. There are fewer white blood cells in the body than red blood cells, but they are larger. They can change shape as they pass across capillary walls to reach where they are needed. White blood cells respond to emergencies, multiplying to fight any infection.

Superheroes

There are three main types of white blood cells: lymphocytes, granulocytes and monocytes.

Lymphocytes produce chemicals called antibodies. These can destroy viruses and bacteria. They also attack fungi and cancer cells. When an infection disappears, the white blood cells sometimes 'remember' the antibody it produced in order to fight the infection. This protects the body next time the same enemy invades.

Granulocytes sweep through the body, changing shape and then swallowing up any unwelcome bacteria. They also remove cell debris.

Monocytes detect the presence of infection and swarm to the site, multiplying and enlarging themselves. Then they digest the unwelcome bacteria.

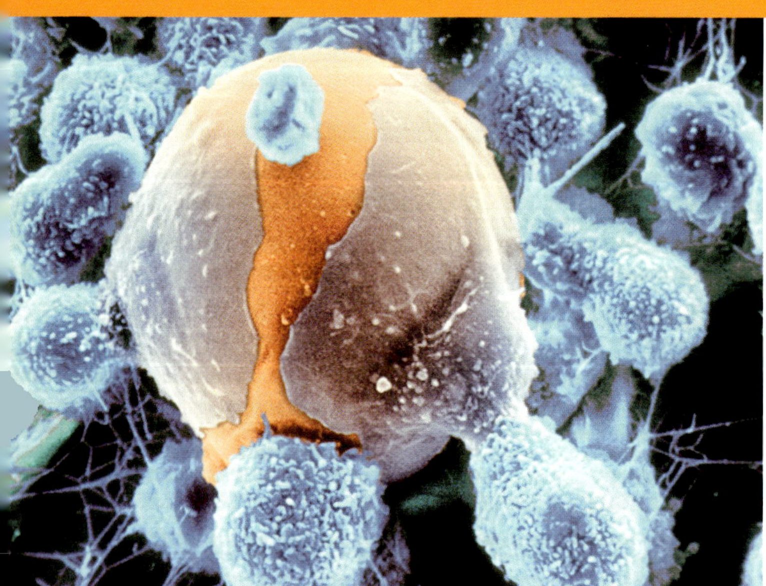

White blood cells (coloured blue in this electronically magnified image) surround and destroy an invading germ.

Attacking cells

HIV (Human Immunodeficiency Virus) is a virus that attacks lymphocytes. Because lymphocytes are important in fighting off germs, this leaves the body vulnerable to illness. Infection from the HIV virus can lead to the condition called AIDS (Acquired Immunodeficiency Syndrome), which can be fatal.

The HIV virus can be passed from mothers to their unborn children. HIV can also be passed on when an infected person has unprotected sex or shares needles with other people when injecting drugs into the body. Treatments are now available in some parts of the world that can delay HIV developing into AIDS, but as yet there is no cure for HIV infection or AIDS.

Body facts

Animals' immune systems are sometimes used to detect germs in humans. The National Aeronautics and Space Administration (NASA) uses horseshoe crabs' blood to detect germs in their space shuttles. The blood of the horseshoe crab changes colour when bacteria are present. Astronauts check the shuttle is germ-free with a hand-held device containing the crab's blood. A sample of an astronaut's blood can also be placed in the device. The crab's blood reacts if the astronaut has an infection.

Cuts and bruises

The cell fragments in your blood called platelets also help to heal the body. If you cut your knee, platelets rush to the wound. There, the platelets swell up and become sticky so that they can plug the hole. They trap other blood cells that are about to leak out of the hole in the skin. When the platelets dry up, they form a protective scab at the surface of the skin.

If you fall and hurt your knee, you may break some blood capillaries under the skin, without breaking the skin itself. The blood that leaks out of the capillaries collects under the surface of the skin, forming a purple or blue mark known as a bruise. This is often sore to touch.

This small device contains tiny parts from a horseshoe crab's blood. It enables astronauts to analyse blood samples in about five minutes.

Blood types

Each of us has a particular type of blood, characterised by the presence of certain proteins. There are four blood types, each of which is determined before birth by your genetic make-up – the characteristics you inherit from your parents. The four blood types are: A, B, AB and O.

A or B?

When a sperm fertilises an egg, the newly formed embryo inherits a gene from the mother and a gene from the father which determine the blood type. These genes make proteins that are present on the surface of each of the trillions of red blood cells in the body. The proteins on the red blood cells create a fighting mechanism – antibodies – to fight off proteins from different blood groups. For example, a person with blood group A has proteins that would reject blood cells from blood group B. Doctors need to know patients' blood types so that their bodies will not reject blood that is given in a transfusion.

When a blood sample is sent to a laboratory, it is examined under a microscope or tested with chemicals, depending on what is being checked.

Life-saving discoveries

Blood transfusions involve injecting the blood from one person into another. The first attempts at blood transfusions often ended in disaster. Doctors were unaware that there were different types of blood, and that they were not compatible.

However, this changed in the early 20th century when Dr Karl Landsteiner identified different blood groups. After this discovery, blood transfusions began to save people's lives, although only fresh blood could be used.

During the First World War (1914-1918), scientists discovered that a chemical called sodium nitrate prevented blood from clotting when it was removed from a body. They also found that storing the blood in a fridge kept it fresh. These discoveries saved the lives of thousands of wounded soldiers.

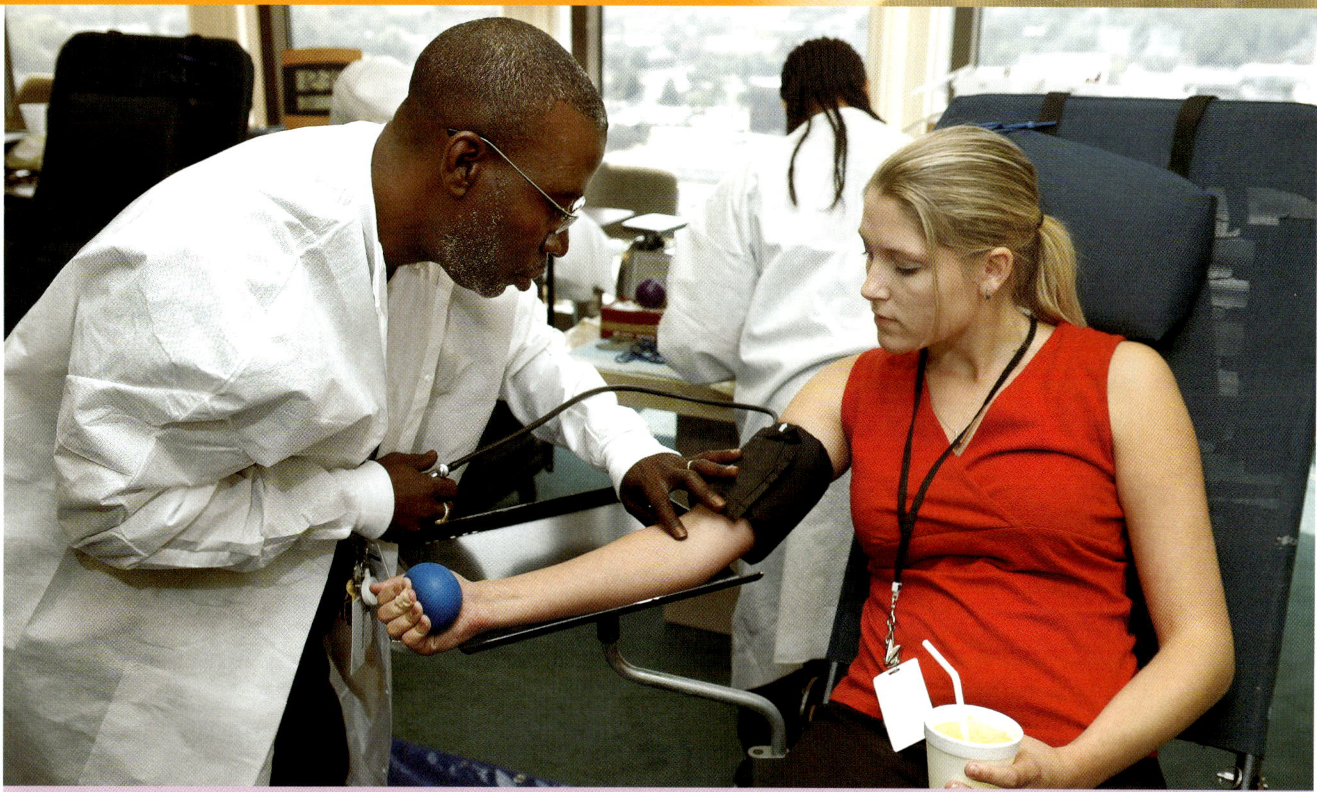

This health care worker is preparing to draw blood from a blood donor. Her blood will be stored in a blood bank and may be used in a blood transfusion.

Breaking up blood

The blood is an important tool for diagnosing and monitoring health. A blood sample can reveal a lot about a person's health. In a laboratory, specially trained technicians analyse blood samples. They pass them through special machines or examine them closely under a microscope.

Detective work

A speck of blood can help solve a crime. Forensic scientists examine the tiniest specks of blood. The speck can provide details of a person's blood type, any illnesses he or she might have and details of his or her genetic make-up. This information helps the police find out who the blood belongs to. New scientific techniques enable the police to get important information from blood samples taken from the scenes of crimes that were committed more than 30 years ago.

Investigate

Make a bar chart listing the main blood types. Ask a sample of ten people (male and female) which blood group each one belongs to. Note down their age, sex and country of birth. Record the results on the chart. Can you find any pattern relating to age, sex or country of birth?

Waste disposal

Blood does a lot of fetching and carrying of different substances from food, drink and chemical processes in the cells. When the cells take delivery of nutrients, such as proteins from food, they break them down in a chemical process. This process creates waste, such as water and carbon dioxide. The waste is carried away in the blood which returns to the heart and then the lungs. The blood needs a good clean – and it gets it, several times a day.

Liver stop

After you've eaten something, the vitamins, minerals and other nutrients from the food pass from the intestine into the blood. Before going out to the rest of the body, blood that is rich with nutrients from food passes through the liver. The liver stocks up on fats, glucose and carbohydrates. It releases these back into the blood when needed.

Liver cleanse

The liver also cleans the blood, taking out and breaking down harmful chemicals and substances, such as those in alcohol. The liver packs them off in a substance called bile. The bile is sent to the intestines through a tube called the bile duct. The waste products in the bile leave the body in solid waste matter called faeces.

▼ This diagram shows the main organs involved in cleaning the blood.

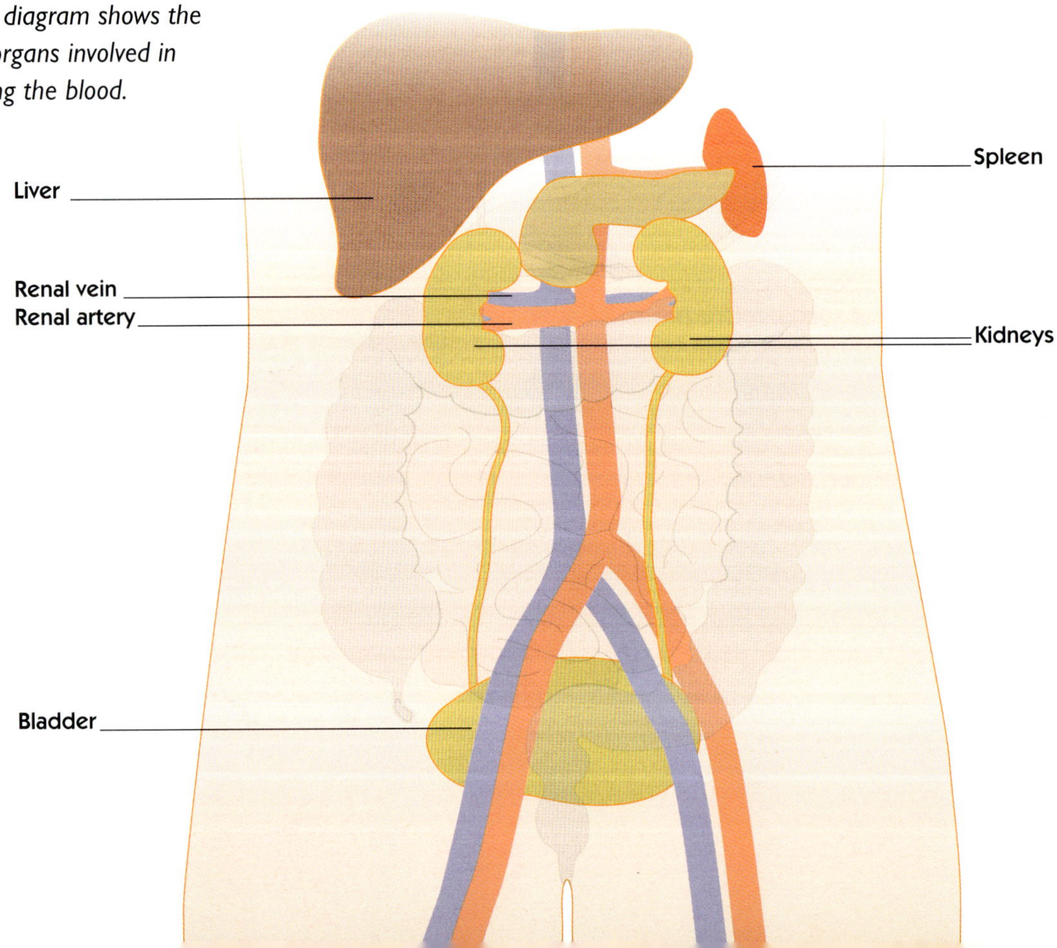

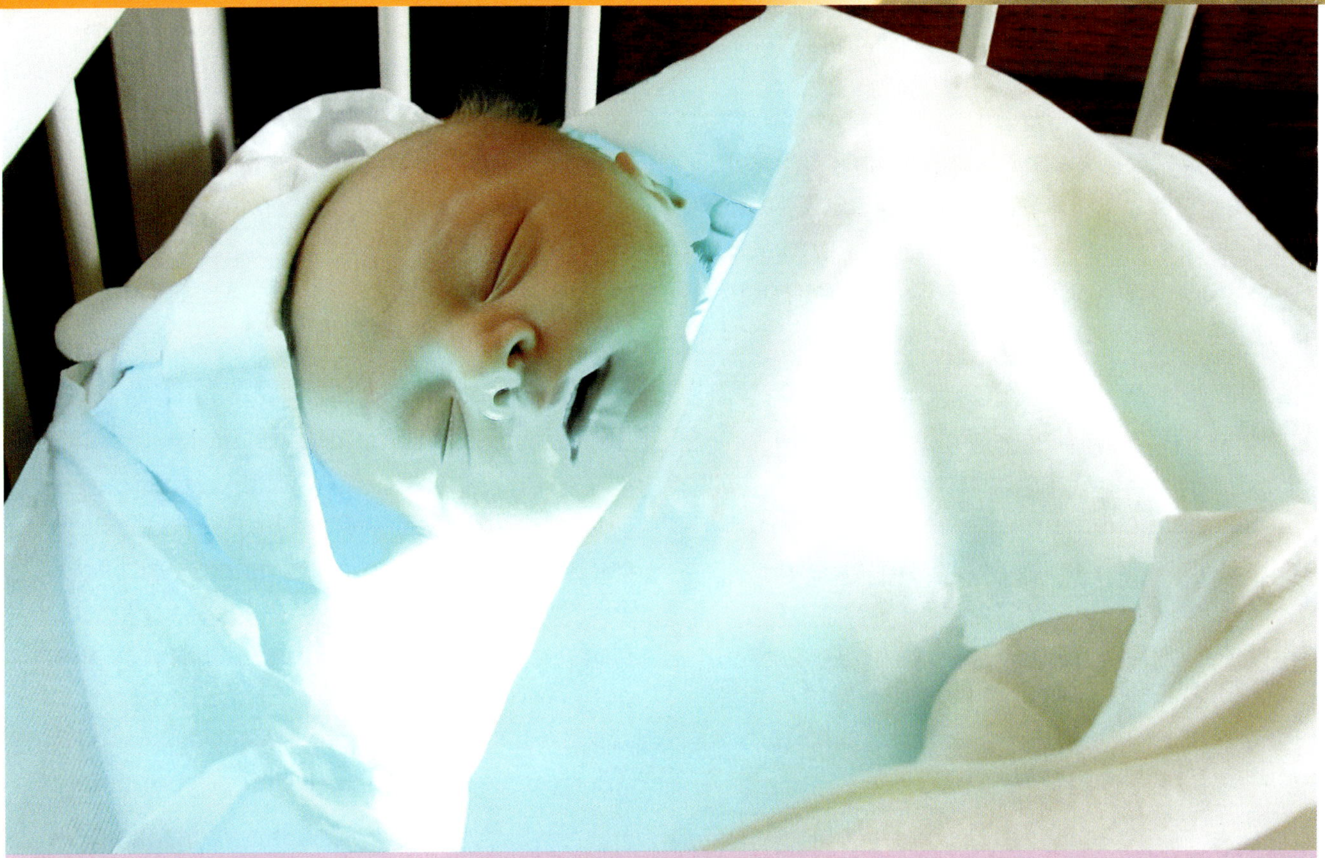

Some babies are born slightly yellow, a condition called jaundice. This is caused by too much bilirubin, a waste product from red blood cells. In babies, this is treated by placing them under special lights that break down the bilirubin.

Kidney cleanse

The kidneys make sure that blood contains the right balance of water and salts. Any waste that the kidneys filter from the blood is excreted through the body in urine. Blood enters the kidneys through the renal artery and, once cleansed, moves back towards the heart through the renal vein.

Bloody factory

From an unborn baby to an elderly person, the human body is constantly making, breaking down and reusing blood cells. Before a baby is born, red blood cells form in the bone marrow, liver, spleen and lymph nodes. In children, the blood cells form in the bone marrow – the soft tissue in the centre of bones. In adults, blood cells are only produced in the bone marrow of certain bones, such as the pelvis, chest bone and vertebrae.

A white blood cell lasts for between one to four days and a platelet lives for about one week. After about 120 days, the red blood cells wear out and eventually die. Every second, 2.5 million red blood cells are broken down, but the body is continually producing new ones. The spleen and liver break down ageing blood cells. Iron from the haemoglobin is stored in the liver where it is reused by newly-formed blood cells. The rest of the haemoglobin is used to form bile in the liver.

The cardiovascular system

Your heart is tireless. It beats continuously and regularly, only ever pausing for a fraction of a second. Without the action of your heart, blood stops flowing and your body stops working. The heart is the motor of the cardiovascular system.

Muscle power

The heart lies on the left-hand side of the body, protected by the breastbone. It is a muscle, the movement of which is regulated by the heart's own internal electrical system (see pages 22-23). This tells your heart when to beat without you having to think about it. Cardiac (heart) muscle is different from other muscles in your body. Unlike them, cardiac muscle never gets tired.

Left and right

The heart is made up of two pumps (the left and right), which perform different functions. The right-hand side of the heart pumps blood to the lungs where it picks up oxygen. The left-hand side of the heart pumps oxygenated blood from the lungs, around the rest of the body. A wall of muscle called the septum separates the two sides, preventing blood from the right side mixing with blood from the left.

▼ *This diagram shows the heart's four chambers, the two upper atria and two lower ventricles.*

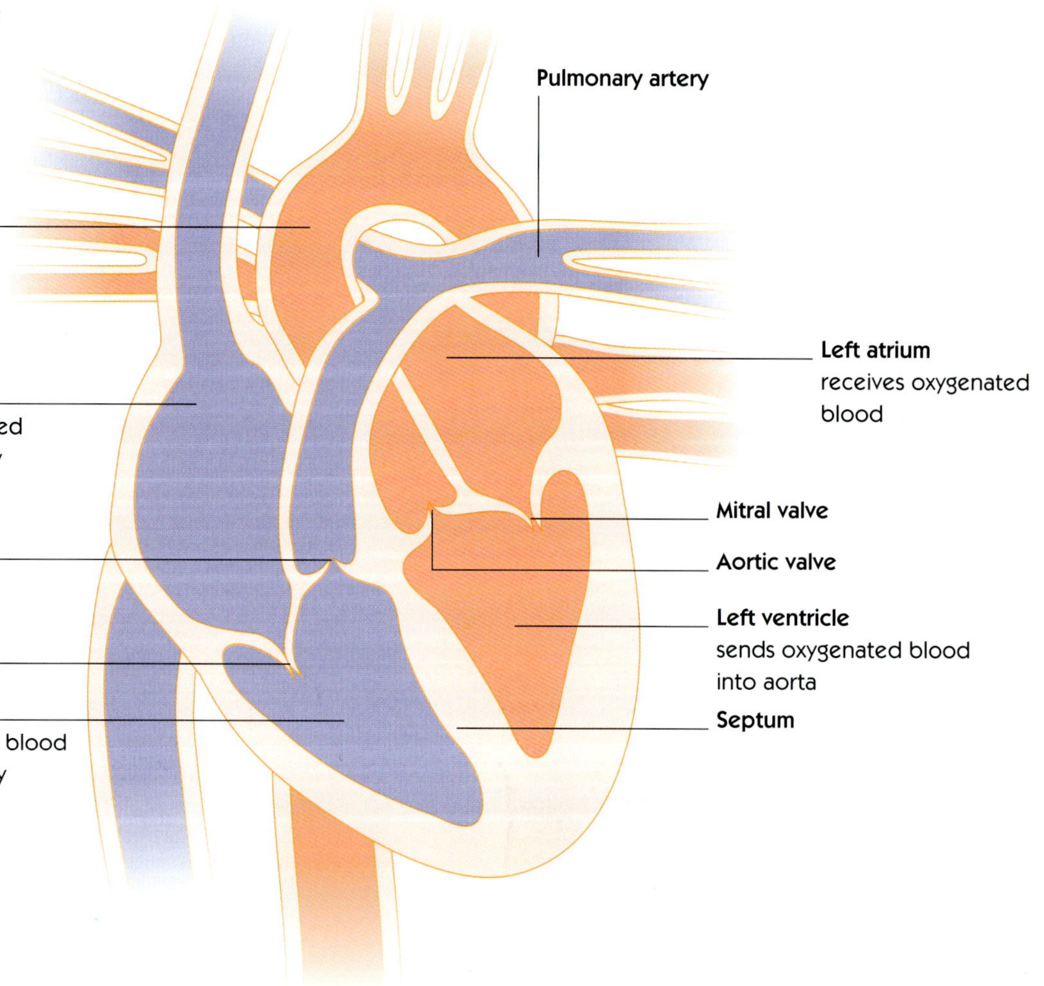

Top and bottom

Each side of the heart is divided into two chambers. The top chamber is called the atrium and the bottom chamber is the ventricle. The ventricle walls are thicker and more muscular than the atria walls because ventricles have to pump blood around the body. But the right ventricle only sends blood through the lungs, so its walls are not as thick as the walls of the left ventricle, which drives blood around the whole body.

One-way traffic

Your heart uses four valves to ensure your blood flows only in one direction. Valves open and close in coordination with the pumping action of the heart's atria and ventricles. Each valve has a set of flaps that seals or opens the valves. This allows pumped blood to pass through the chambers and into your blood vessels without backing up or flowing backwards.

Investigate

The heart in humans and other vertebrates (animals with a backbone) pumps blood around the body via blood vessels. Is the heart structure the same for other groups of animals? Choose one animal from the amphibian, reptile and insect groups. How does the heart work in each animal? Compare and contrast the different heart structures and summarise your findings on a chart.

The heart constantly pumps blood around the body, even when you sleep.

Heartbeat

A heart beats about 3 billion times in a lifetime. The beat is the contracting and relaxing mechanism of the heart which pumps blood around the body. The beat can speed up and slow down, according to what a person is doing. But if the beating stops for too long, then the rest of the body ceases to work.

In a beat

In less than one second (that's just one heartbeat in a healthy adult) the following events take place. First, deoxygenated blood fills the right atrium at the same time as oxygenated blood enters the left atrium. Then the atria squeeze together (contract), forcing blood into the ventricles. Finally, the ventricles contract. This forces the deoxygenated blood into the pulmonary artery and the oxygenated blood into the aorta.

Between each contraction, the heart muscle relaxes. The contraction of the heart muscle is called systole. Relaxation of the heart muscle is called diastole.

Listen to the beat

Put your head against someone's chest and you can probably hear the rhythmic beat of the heart – it sounds like 'lub' 'dub'. The first sound 'lub' is the valves slamming shut so that blood cannot flow back from the ventricles into the

▼1) Right atrium fills with deoxygenated blood (blue) while left atrium fills with oxygenated blood (red). Valves remain shut.

▼2) The two atria contract to squeeze blood into the ventricles. The valves between the atria and ventricles are open.

▼3) Both ventricles contract. Blood is forced from the left ventricle into the aorta, and from the right ventricle into the pulmonary artery. The valves between the ventricles and the aorta and pulmonary artery are open.

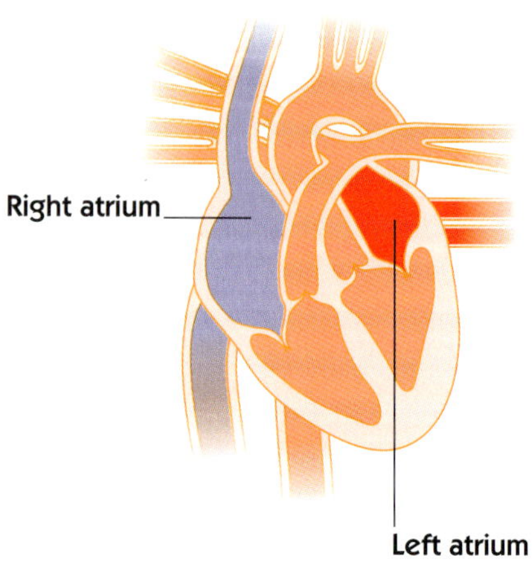

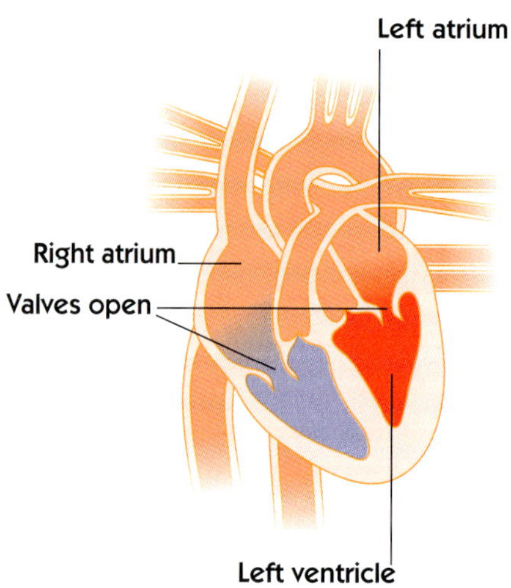

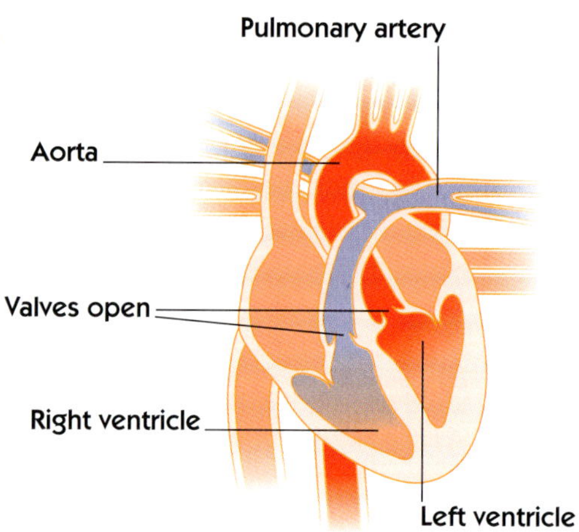

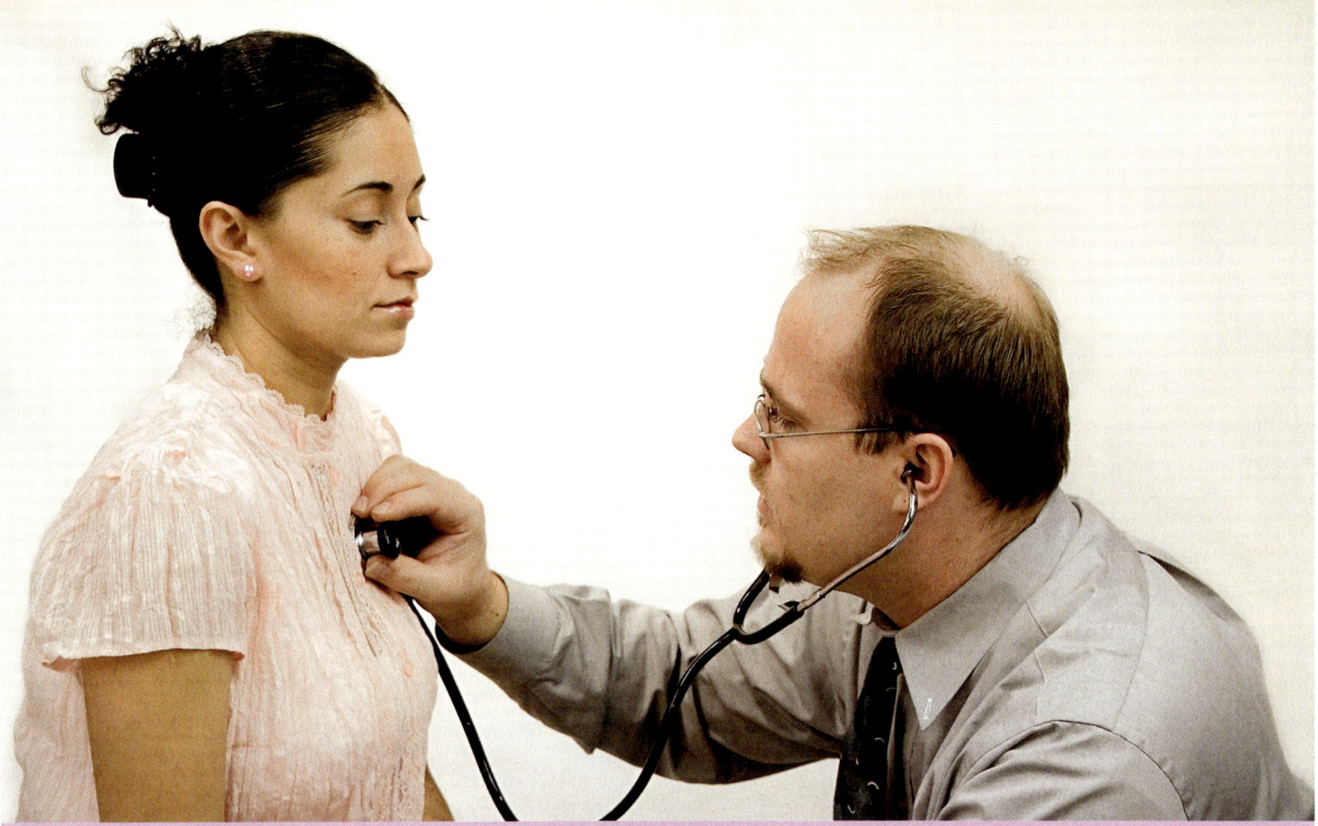

Doctors use a stethoscope to listen clearly to the heartbeat. Extra or unusual sounds, such as a whooshing or swishing noise, can indicate a problem with the heart's pumping action or with the closing of the valves.

atria. The second sound 'dub' is the noise of the valves in the arteries closing to prevent blood flowing back from the arteries into the ventricles.

Private supply

The coronary arteries are blood vessels that wrap around the outside of the heart, bringing the heart its own supply of oxygen-rich blood. Coronary veins carry away the deoxygenated blood. This is called the coronary system.

Waves of blood

As the heart contracts, the pressure at which it forces out blood is at its highest. As the heart relaxes, the pressure drops. You can feel your pulse, or the squeezing and relaxing of the artery, as it responds to the pumping action of the heart.

Heart swap

The first successful heart transplant took place in 1967, performed by a South African doctor called Christiaan Barnard. He transplanted the healthy heart of a woman who had died in a car accident into the body of a man with a damaged heart. The man only survived for 18 days, but the operation proved that it could be done.

Today, thousands of heart transplants are carried out each year and patients survive for many years, thanks to improved drugs and advances in medical techniques. Technology now allows doctors to keep a human heart beating outside the body for up to 12 hours before transplanting it into another human.

The heart's timekeeper

An electrical system in the heart regulates and powers the pumping system. It is a bit like the wiring in a house which allows the central heating or lights to work.

Electrical signals

Each beat of your heart is kick-started by an electrical signal or impulse from within your heart muscle. In a healthy heart, the beat begins with a signal from the sino-atrial node (see below). The signal travels across the heart's top chambers (the atria), then through a group of cells called the atria-ventricular node. This group of cells lies between the atria and the ventricles and acts like a junction box. The electrical impulse then travels through the ventricles. The heart starts to contract and relax before it pumps again.

Sino-atrial node

The sino-atrial node (sometimes just called SA node) is made up of a group of cells and lies at the top of the right atrium. It is your heart's natural pacemaker, coordinating the rate or speed of the heartbeat. Your pulse, or heart rate, is the number of signals the sino-atrial node produces per minute.

Pacemaker

Sometimes, the heart's electrical system is faulty. It causes the heart to beat too quickly or too slowly, making a person feel dizzy or faint. To correct the condition, doctors insert an artificial pacemaker. This is a battery with an electronic circuit, connected to the heart by leads. The pacemaker monitors the action of the heart and produces electrical rhythms to replace any abnormal rhythms.

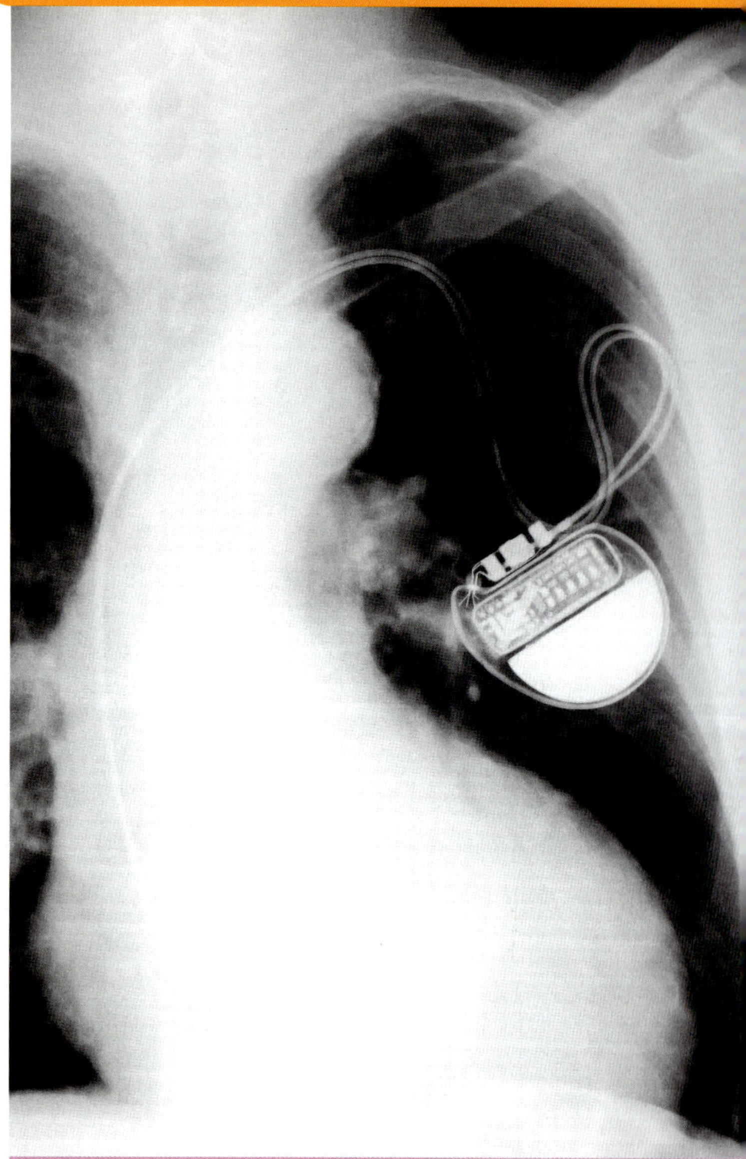

This is an x-ray of a chest showing a pacemaker in position. This device is the size of a large coin and can be inserted in adults or even newborn babies.

Changing pace

Sometimes you can hear and feel the thud of your heartbeat, an action which usually goes unnoticed. This often happens when you exercise or when you are feeling very anxious. Your heart does not know you are feeling anxious – but your brain does. Your brain relays messages, such as fear or anxiety, to the rest of the body, signalling the heart to pump more oxygenated blood around the body more quickly – just in case you need to make a run for it!

Body facts

A baby's heartbeat is much faster than an adult's. It beats at about 140 beats per minute. The average heartbeat of an adult is about 70-75 beats per minute. An elephant's heart beats at about 25 beats per minute, while a tiny canary's heart beats at about 1,000 beats per minute.

Some people feel their heartbeat increase in speed when they are very nervous, for example when they are taking an exam!

Keeping the heart healthy

The heart is often associated with love and feelings, but in fact it is only concerned with keeping the body alive. You cannot consciously control the action of the heart but you can do plenty of things to keep it in good shape. A healthy heart supports other organs. For example, if the heart does not efficiently send enough oxygen to the brain, brain cells begin to die and this results in brain damage.

Work it

The heart is a muscle. It goes flabby and weak if it is not exercised. To keep it strong, it needs regular exercise that makes you feel out of breath (only do this if you are fit and healthy to begin with, otherwise check with your doctor first). The blood in the artery is already packed with oxygen – it can't carry more and the body can't store oxygen. The only way to get more oxygen to the working muscles is for the heart to pump blood around more quickly. To do this, the heart must work harder.

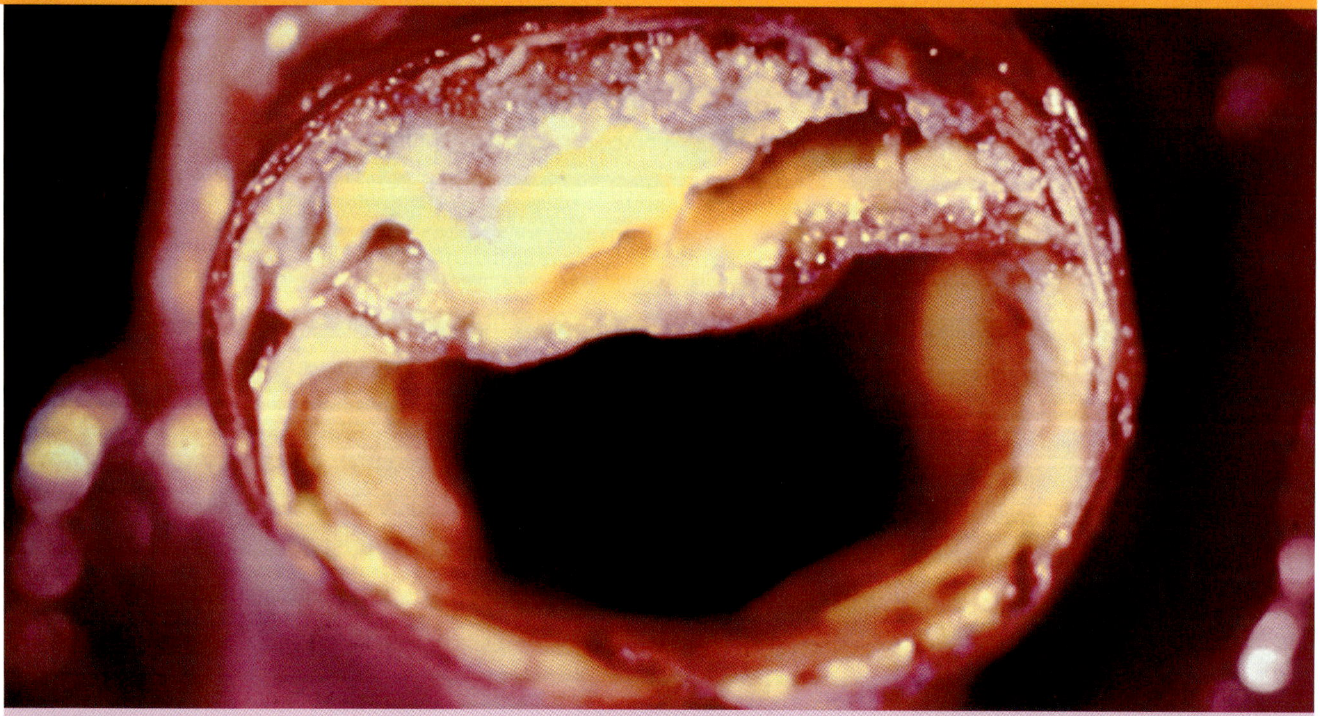

This magnified image shows an artery with a thick fatty deposit (top). The deposit makes the artery narrower and restricts blood flow.

Under pressure

Have you ever had your blood pressure checked? The nurse or doctor puts a tight band around your arm and measures your blood pressure. Blood pressure is the force of blood pushing against the walls of the arteries and it is recorded as two numbers. The first number represents the systolic pressure (the contraction of your heart); the second number represents the diastolic pressure (when the heart relaxes between beats).

High blood pressure can cause the heart to become enlarged or weak and can lead to serious health problems. Eating less salt, exercising regularly and having a healthy diet can all keep blood pressure at a healthy level.

Fatty foods

Crisps, biscuits and cakes may taste delicious, but they are often full of fats. Some fats are essential for healthy cell growth. However, too much fat in your diet can lead to blockages in the arteries and then heart problems. Sometimes, the coronary arteries become narrower with a build-up of fatty material caused by eating too many fatty foods.

The coronary arteries bring the heart its own blood supply. When they become narrower, not enough blood can reach the heart muscle. Without enough blood, the heart muscle is starved of oxygen and part of it dies. This can lead to a heart attack. Allowing yourself fatty foods only as occasional treats can help keep the heart healthy.

Investigate

Heart disease is one of the most common causes of death in some countries today. Investigate which countries have the highest instances of heart disease and which have the fewest. Look at lifestyle issues, diet and other factors in these countries to draw reasons for your findings.

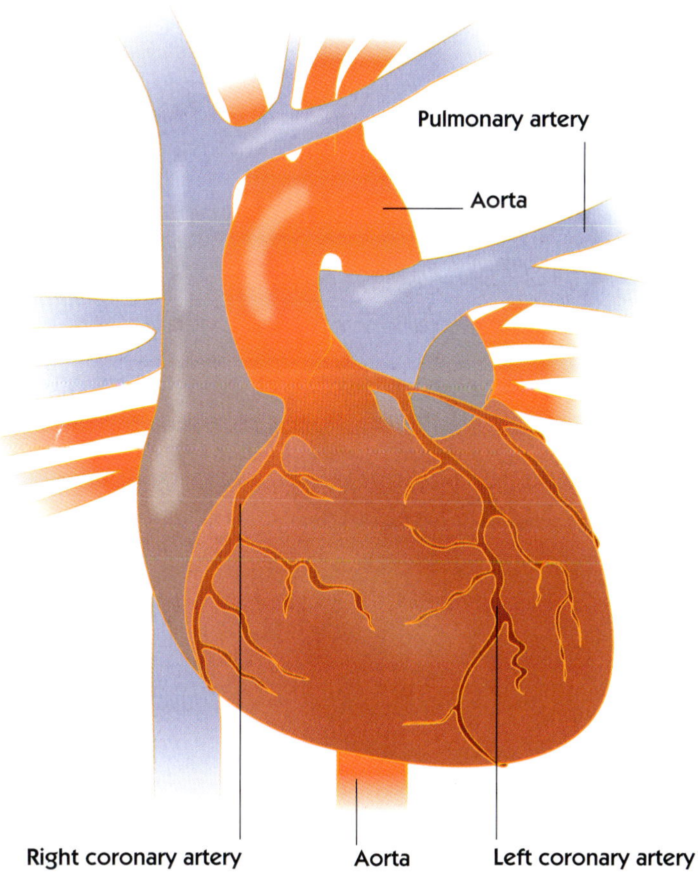

▲ *Coronary arteries branch off the aorta and provide the heart with its own blood supply.*

Keeping blood healthy

What you eat goes into your blood. Eating well helps blood flow freely and efficiently around the body. This helps the heart to remain strong, muscular and fully active.

Drink up!

Your blood is over 80 per cent water. If you don't drink enough water, your blood becomes thicker and moves around the body more sluggishly. Then it's harder to concentrate and you feel more tired.

Water helps the liver and kidneys get rid of toxins (harmful substances). Drinking cola, tea or coffee doesn't do the job of pure water because these drinks contain caffeine. Caffeine is a substance that stimulates or speeds up the central nervous system – the parts of the body responsible for sending messages around the body. Drinks containing caffeine make you lose water rather than keep it.

Drink plenty of water when you exercise. This will ensure you replace the water your body loses through the extra exertion and sweating.

It is possible to drink too much water. When this happens, the blood becomes too diluted and then the brain doesn't receive enough salt.

Cool it!

The heart and blood work together to keep the body's temperature within a certain range, whether the temperature is blisteringly hot or icy cold outside the body.

When you are too hot, the blood vessels in your skin expand (dilate) and carry the excess heat to the surface of the skin. This is why you may look red after strenuous exercise, when the body gets hotter. If you are too cold, the blood vessels contract and narrow to reduce blood flow around the body. This preserves the body's heat.

Fatty blood

Cholesterol is a waxy, fatty substance carried in the blood. A certain amount is essential for the working of all the cells in the body. The body makes its own cholesterol, but this waxy substance is also found in many foods that you eat. Too much cholesterol can lead to heart problems. It clogs up the blood vessels, preventing oxygen-rich blood cells from passing through. This can result in a heart attack.

Investigate

Do you ever feel a bit dizzy when you stand up suddenly? This can happen because the blood has to fight its way back up your body, defying gravity. Find out what happens when a person faints, and why they fall to the ground.

Put your feet up!

All the hard work of the heart and blood circulation takes its toll on the veins in your legs. As people get older, the valves sometimes begin to wear out. This means that some blood stays in a vein instead of moving onwards and upwards. This makes the vein swell up, and that swollen vein is a called a varicose vein. Keeping active and not standing still for long periods can help prevent varicose veins.

A person whose job involves long periods of standing, like this hairdresser, should move from leg to leg to keep their circulation moving swiftly.

The respiratory system

You can live without food for about a week and without water for a few days. You can only go without breathing air in and out for a few minutes. Breathing is just one action carried out by the respiratory system, but it is the only one you can feel.

What makes us breathe?

Your whole body needs oxygen to survive, but oxygen cannot pass into the blood through the skin. The respiratory system operates a complex transfer of oxygen from the air outside your body, into your blood and then to the cells. It also gets rid of the waste product carbon dioxide. The cardiovascular system transports the oxygen and carbon dioxide around the blood.

Investigate

Oxygen is crucial for life. Without it, the body breaks down. Each tissue and cell in the body needs a supply of oxygen. In high mountainous areas, the air is thinner than it is near sea level and there is less oxygen in the air. Find out how people who live in high mountainous areas cope with the lack of oxygen. Do visitors to these environments cope in a similar way?

◀ The respiratory system uses organs in the face, and some beneath the chest.

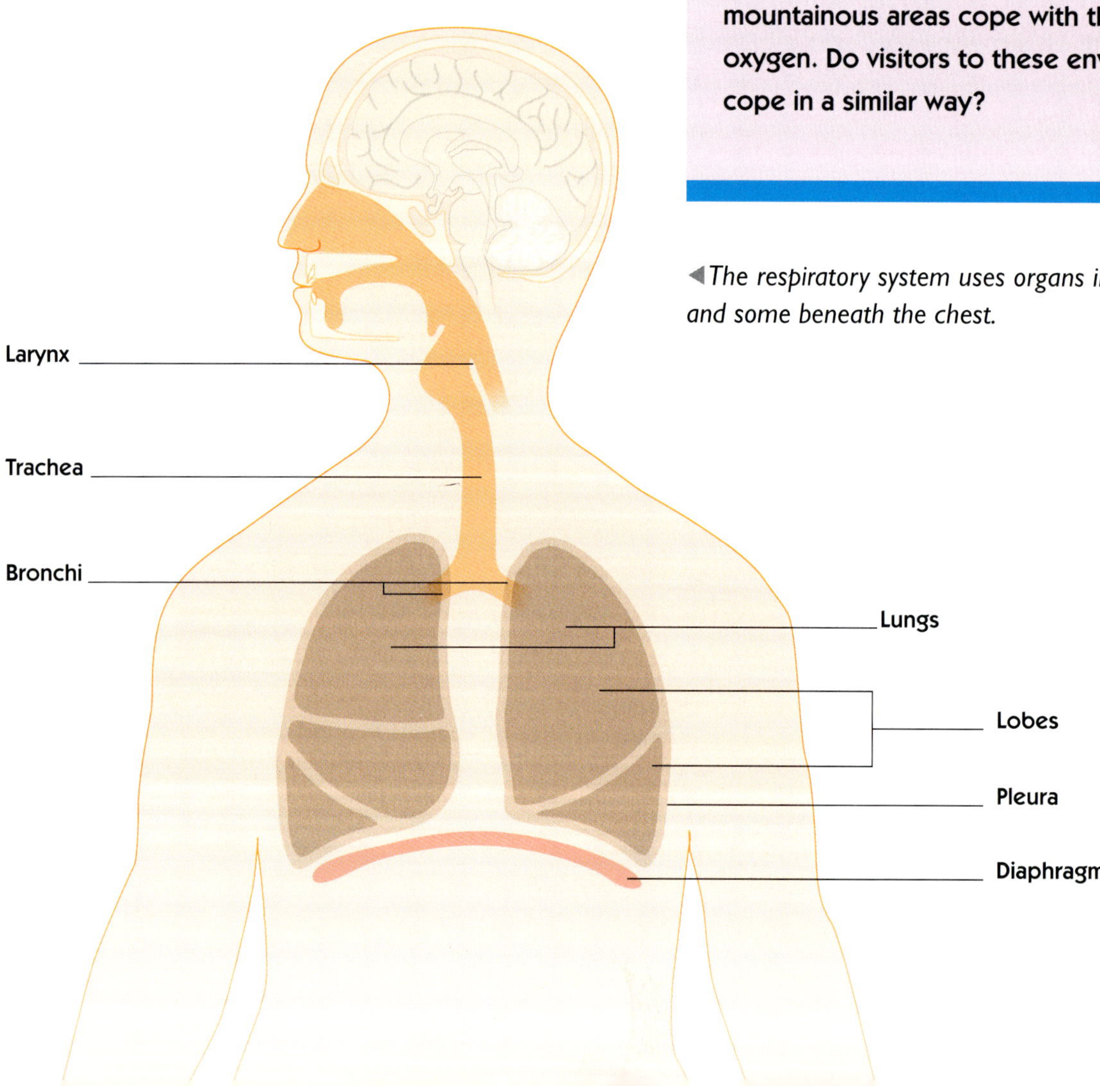

Looking at lungs

You have two lungs, each one weighing about 0.45 kilograms (1 pound). They are one of the largest organs in your body. Lungs are rounded, pink, spongy and inflatable – they can fill up like balloons.

The bony rib cage protects the lungs. The left lung is squashed up next to the heart and is slightly smaller than the right lung. The left lung has two lobes (areas) and the right lung has three lobes. Each lung is covered in tissue or membrane called pleura. This covering helps the lungs change shape when you breathe in and out.

Inside the lungs

Inside, the lungs look like an upside-down tree with a maze of branching tubes. The largest branches are the bronchi. These carry air into and out of the lungs. They branch off into bronchioles that carry air into the alveoli. Alveoli are very thin-walled sacs, or bags, surrounded by thin capillaries. The capillaries are so thin that the blood cells can only pass through them one at a time.

Body facts

There are around 300 million alveoli in each lung. If they were spread out, they would cover a whole tennis court!

If all the blood capillaries in the lungs were laid end to end, they would extend for 1,600 kilometres (994 miles).

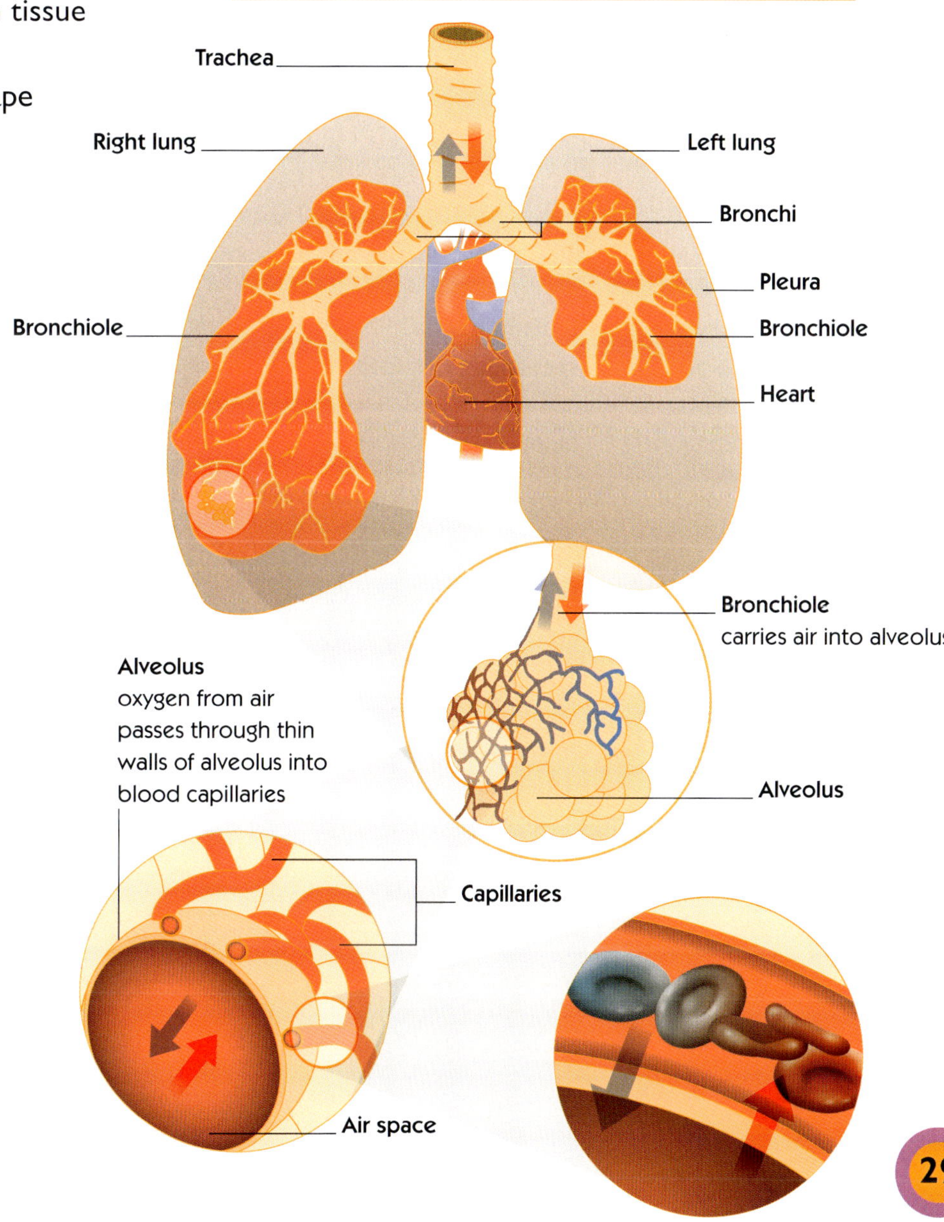

▶ *Inside the lungs is a network of bronchi, bronchioles, alveoli and capillaries. Oxygen in the alveoli passes out into blood in the surrounding capillaries. Carbon dioxide from the blood passes into the alveoli and is expelled in an out breath.*

External respiration

External respiration is the physical process of inhalation and exhalation, more commonly known as breathing. The inflation and deflation of the lungs draws air into and out of the body. This supplies the blood with oxygen and gets rid of carbon dioxide.

Breathe in

Air carrying oxygen is drawn through the nose or mouth where it is warmed and moistened. It passes down the trachea, or windpipe. The diaphragm (a sheet of muscle underneath the lungs) and the rib muscles contract, forcing the ribs upwards and outwards. Next the diaphragm moves down and flattens. This action stretches the lungs and they enlarge – the slippery pleura helps the lungs change size easily and smoothly. Air is sucked into the enlarged lungs.

▼On an in breath, the diaphragm moves downwards and the rib cage moves upwards and outwards, stretching and enlarging the lungs (below). On an out breath, the diaphragm and rib muscles relax and the lungs shrink in size (right).

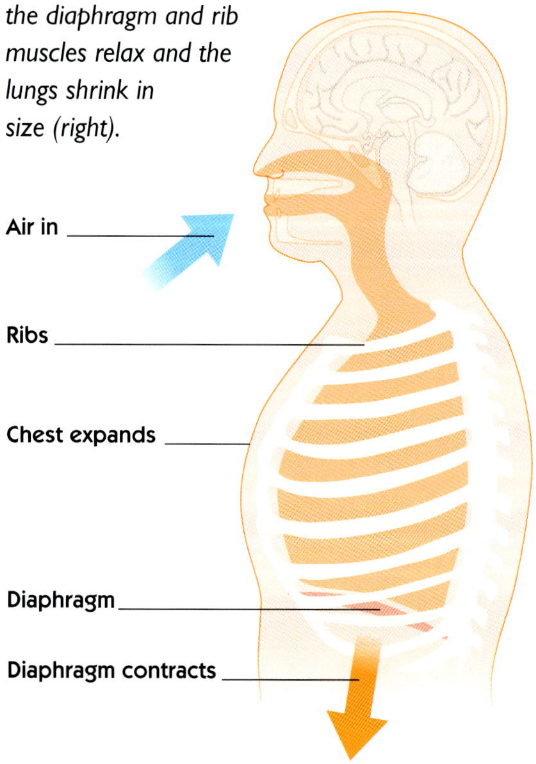

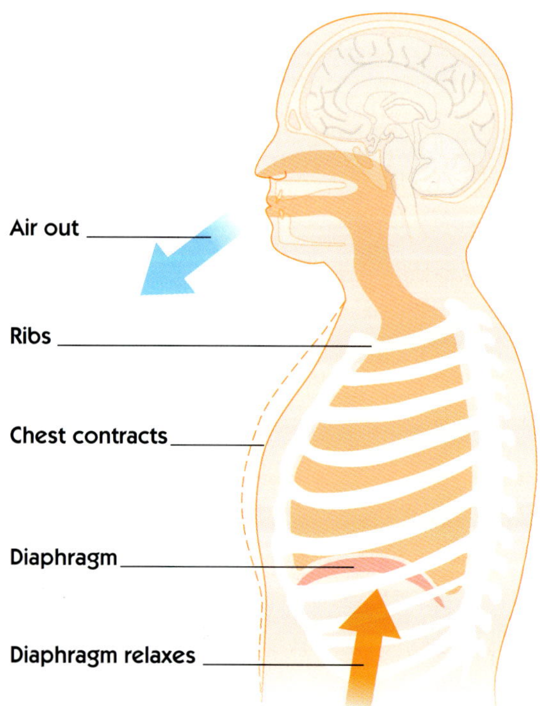

Breathe out

The rib muscles and diaphragm relax. The elastic lungs spring back to their original shape. Air carrying carbon dioxide is pushed out or expelled from the lungs. It passes out of the body into the air in an exhaled breath.

Yawn!

People often yawn when they feel tired or bored. A yawn happens because the breathing has slowed down and there is too much carbon dioxide in the body – the breath responds to levels of carbon dioxide in the blood. A long, stretching yawn opens your

Humans cannot extract oxygen from water, so divers rely on breathing equipment while underwater.

mouth and lungs so that you can take in a gulp of oxygen to wake up a sluggish system and expel the carbon dioxide.

Underwater

Not all animals have lungs. Fish use gills to breathe. Water (containing oxygen) passes through the gills and the oxygen in the water passes into the fish's blood vessels. There is oxygen in water, but humans are not able to breathe underwater without special breathing equipment. This is because the human body is not able to extract oxygen from water.

All talk

The sounds you make as you speak, sing, whisper or shout are created by parts of the respiratory system. Vocal cords across the larynx, or voice box, vibrate as air passes over them and this produces sound. The movement of the tongue and lips turns the sounds into words.

Try this

We normally take shallow breaths using only a small percentage of our lung capacity. Place a hand on each side of your rib cage and breathe normally. Feel how your ribs hardly move. Now, keeping your hands on your rib cage, breathe deeply without raising your shoulders. You should be able to feel your ribs expanding more to make space for the air you have breathed in.

Internal respiration

From the lungs, oxygen crosses the thin walls of the alveoli. Here it is carried away in the blood to the cells for a gas exchange, as oxygen is swapped for carbon dioxide. The carbon dioxide is carried back to the alveoli and then expelled on an out breath. Meanwhile, the oxygen is involved in internal respiration. This is a chemical process during which energy is produced so that all the cells and tissues in the body can carry out their functions.

Food is fuel

The body's energy comes from internal respiration. This is when oxygen is used to break down food substances, such as glucose. Internal respiration releases the energy stored in the food and the cells use this energy to carry out their jobs. The main work is done by mitochondria, tiny structures inside each cell that create energy from nutrients in a chemical process. A muscle cell can contain thousands of these structures, because a muscle needs lots of energy when it is in use.

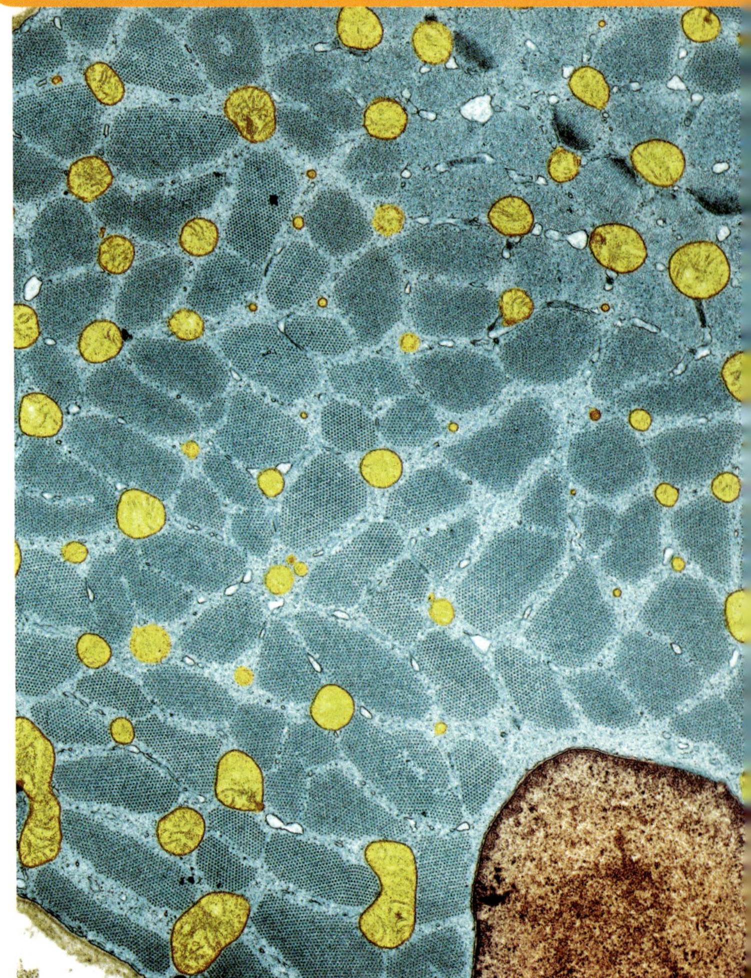

This magnified image shows a cell in a muscle. The yellow marks are mitochondria which produce energy needed by the cell. Mitochondria are known as the cells' powerhouses.

Body facts

The brain, which is only about 2 per cent of the body's weight, receives about 20 per cent of the oxygen that is carried in your blood. Brain cells die if they are deprived of oxygen.

In outer space, where there is no or little atmosphere with oxygen, a person who is not wearing a spacesuit could lose consciousness within 15 seconds because of the lack of oxygen.

Try this

Test yourself on what you know about the respiratory and cardiovascular systems. Draw an outline of a human body. Add in the lungs, heart and major circulatory patterns. Now, in red pen, draw arrows to show the path of an inhaled breath in external respiration (air entering and leaving the lungs). Show the path the oxygen takes to arrive at a cell in the thigh muscle. Describe what happens to the oxygen in that cell. In blue, draw the return route of carbon dioxide.

Carbon dioxide and water are produced as waste products. The blood carries them away from the cells. Carbon dioxide and water vapour are expelled in the out breath, as part of the process of external respiration. Water is excreted in the urine.

Plants

Plants breathe, but, unlike humans, they don't have lungs or a bloodstream. They breathe through holes underneath their leaves called stomata. Plants breathe in carbon dioxide from the air through the stomata. This passes into the plant's cells. Plants use carbon dioxide and water to turn the Sun's energy into food. They release oxygen back into the air – ready for humans to breathe. Without plants and trees, we wouldn't have enough oxygen.

The energy you need to run around and for your body to work, comes from food. But it takes the combined actions of the digestive, respiratory and cardiovascular systems to turn food into usable energy.

Keeping the lungs clean

An incredible 17,000 litres (4,500 gallons) of air move in and out of an adult's lungs every day. Every breath contains healthy oxygen, but it also contains unwelcome germs. There is a lot of dirt in the air, from bits of soot to pollen. Dirt is all around, even if you can't see it.

Filter system

Your body has its own filtering method to protect your lungs and the rest of your internal organs from the dangers of unwanted materials. However, when a person breathes in too many pollutants, the body is unable to filter them all out and the lungs can become damaged.

Sweeping clean

The nose sieves out any unwelcome bits from the air so that they don't harm the delicate branches of the lungs. Sticky mucus lines most of the passages that carry air from the outside into the lungs. It keeps the airways moist and clean, trapping dust and bacteria before it reaches the lungs. Tiny hairs called cilia line the bronchi. They push the mucus away from the lungs. You either cough up the mucus, sneeze it out or swallow it.

Investigate

Healthy lungs look pinkish-grey. Lungs that have become polluted with harmful substances, such as chemicals in cigarettes, have black spots on the surface. Ask a sample of 15 adults their reasons for smoking or not smoking. Design and write a poster to persuade smokers to quit, taking into account the responses to your questions. You could include facts and statistics about the effects of smoking. Think about the kind of imagery you will use – will it be hard-hitting or will you use a more gentle approach?

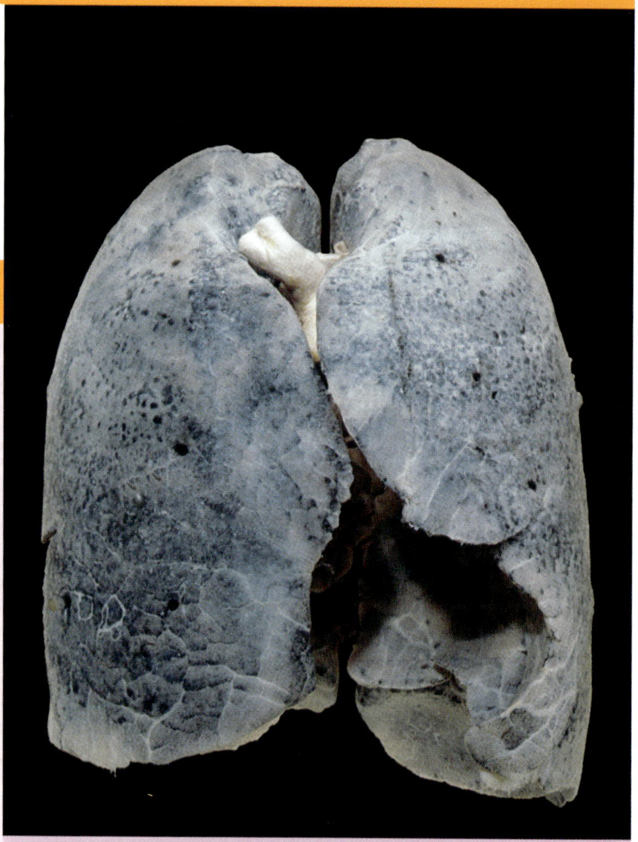

Healthy lungs should be a pinky colour. This picture shows the damaged lungs of a smoker.

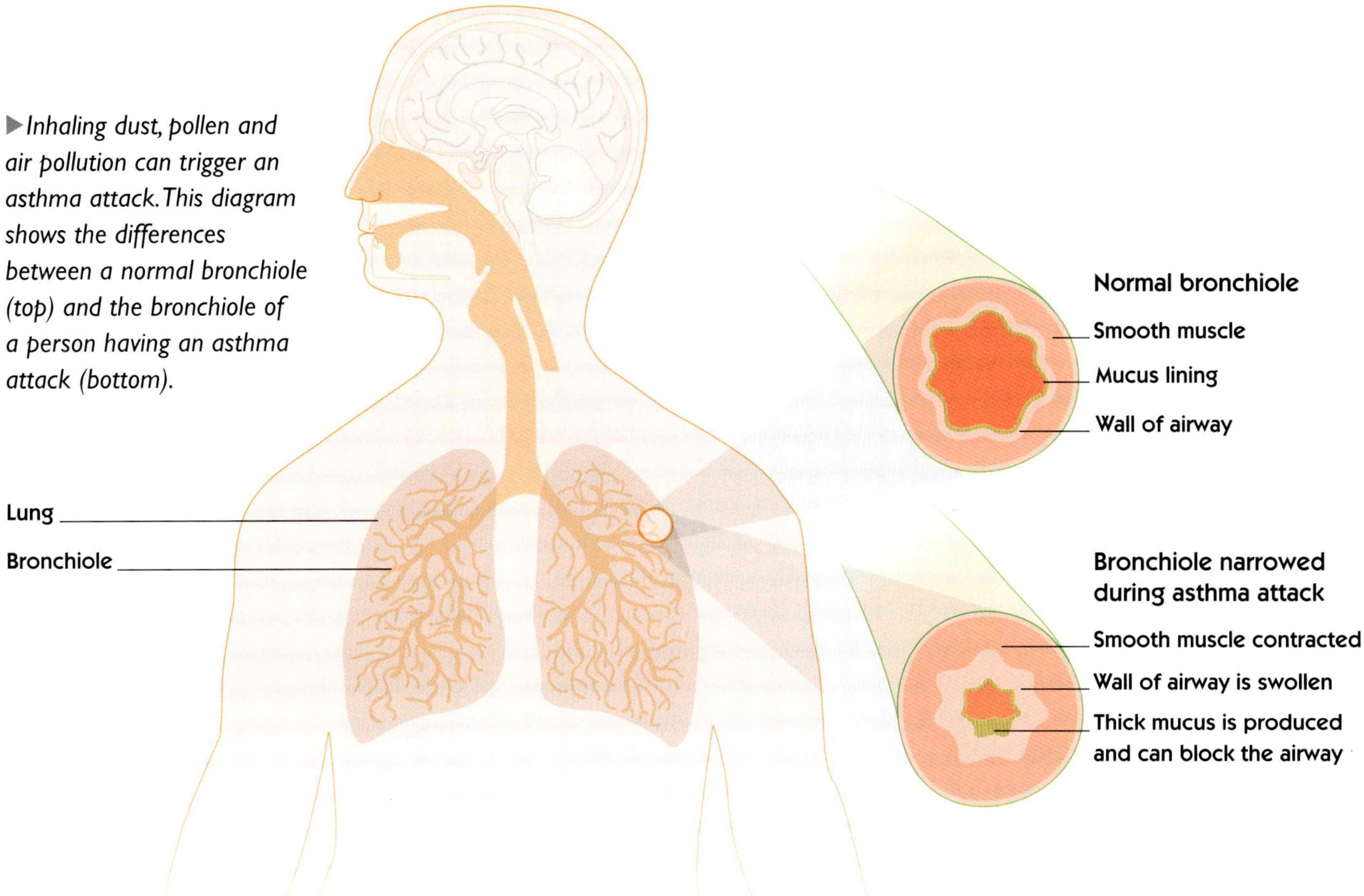

▶ *Inhaling dust, pollen and air pollution can trigger an asthma attack. This diagram shows the differences between a normal bronchiole (top) and the bronchiole of a person having an asthma attack (bottom).*

Cover up!

The body automatically responds to any interference in the throat or trachea. A cough is a blast of air from the lungs which forces out germs and dangerous particles. People put their hands in front of their mouths when they cough or yawn. This is to stop germs from escaping into the air which another person could breathe in.

Dirty air

Indoor pollution causes the death of 1.6 million people every year – that's the death of one person every 20 seconds. One cause is inhaling smoke from burning wood inside a room with little ventilation. Then the soot from the wood clogs up the lungs. In many developing countries wood is often the main source of fuel for heating and cooking. Supplying people with stoves that funnel the soot safely outside would save many lives.

Can't breathe

Asthma is a common breathing difficulty which can affect a person mildly or severely. A substance, such as pollen from flowers, irritates the airways, making the walls of the airways swell and produce extra mucus. Soft muscle surrounds the walls of the airways and during an asthma attack, these muscles contract. These changes narrow the tubes and make the person wheeze and cough. Inhaling special medicines that widen the airways can help to control an asthma attack.

Healthy lungs

You can train your lungs to work harder and more efficiently. This helps them provide more oxygen to the muscles involved in exercise which means the muscles can work harder and for longer. Gradually increasing exercise also helps the lungs to increase their capacity to take in air and life-giving oxygen.

Balloon-like

Healthy lungs are elastic so they can expand when you inhale. Some illnesses, such as emphysema, make lungs lose their elasticity and they cannot expand properly. When this happens, a person has difficulty breathing and tires easily.

Aerobic or anaerobic?

You may have seen aerobics classes advertised at sports and fitness centres. Aerobic exercises, such as jogging, dancing, swimming or football, increase the heart rate over a longer period of time. 'Aerobic' means 'with oxygen', and aerobic exercise uses up oxygen. Anaerobic exercises, such as weightlifting and sprint racing, rely on short bursts of strength. 'Anaerobic' means 'without oxygen'.

Anaerobic respiration

You are about to miss the bus, so you have to run very fast to catch it. To do this, your cells need lots of energy but you can only inhale a certain amount of air. To keep the cells 'burning'

Hurdle jumping uses muscles at a high intensity for a short period of time. This is anaerobic exercise.

It is common for people playing spo[...]mes this is caused by a build up of lactic acid. Stretching c[...]

up energy from glucose, th
sometimes need to conve
without using oxygen. Th
respiration. It produces
that is carried away in

During anaerobic ex
on a lack of oxygen
debt. When you ar
bus, puffing and pa
oxygen to replac
the body.

This oxygen b
down the lac
much lactic aci
may feel a sharp muscle pa

covery time

up energy and the body needs
d into energy quickly. To do this,
d lungs work harder. Your heart
pump extra food and oxygen to
. Breathing speeds up to take in
gen and get rid of more carbon
When a very fit person exercises, his
ulse rate, breathing rate and lactic acid
se, but much less than they do in an unfit
. The body has become fitter and therefore
able to supply oxygen to the cells.

time it takes for a person's pulse and
eathing rate to return to normal is called
e recovery time. The fitter you are, the
horter your recovery time.

Computer Users

Your pin number has changed!

Your new pin will be the first two numbers of your house number and the last two numbers of your postcode

Example: 129 Honeybourne Street postcode B62 4RD Pin = 1224

If your house number is between 1-9 please add a zero before your house number and if you do not have a house number at all please use 00

A working machine

The body is an incredible machine driven by the complex interaction of the heart, blood and lungs. The first thing a doctor checks in an emergency is a person's breathing and heartbeat. Without these, nothing else will work.

Growing up

An unborn child receives the same nutrients as the mother. In the womb, a foetus (unborn baby) receives oxygen and nutrients from the mother's blood supply via the umbilical cord. The baby's blood is linked to the mother's circulatory system. When babies are born, they must start to breathe independently and to rely on their own blood supply. The lungs must start to work. From then on and until the age of about 20, their bodies are developing.

Within moments of birth, a baby takes its first breath and fills its lungs with air. Then the heart, lungs and blood begin their lifelong work.

Growing older

Between the ages of 20 and 80, the arteries become stiffer and thicker, making it harder for blood to flow through them. Making sure that your diet is healthy and exercising a sensible amount will help keep your arteries clear of clogs and keep your blood flowing.

By the age of 20, the lungs' capacity to take in oxygen and breathe out carbon dioxide decreases. Try to do some regular exercise to increase the capacity of your lungs.

Think about it

Without you even having to think about them, your lungs, heart and blood work together to keep you alive.

What happens to you when you sit down with a bowl of popcorn and watch a really scary film? The feelings of fear and anxiety from watching the film signal to the brain to release a chemical called adrenaline into the blood. This prepares the body to be on red alert and ready to react – just in case the film turns real!

Adrenaline causes your heart to beat faster, your blood to pump around more quickly and your rate of breathing to increase. The sugary popcorn is broken down in the digestive system into substances including glucose and carbohydrates. These travel around in the blood. In each cell, they are turned into energy to make your cells work.

Investigate

You don't have to be an Olympic athlete on a strict no-sweets, no-cakes diet to be fit. Keep your heart healthy simply by walking or cycling instead of taking the bus, and eat plenty of healthy foods (together with an occasional treat). Find out which foods are best for keeping your respiratory and cardiovascular systems in top working order. Find out how much and what type of exercise a young person should do to keep fit, well and happy.

Even when you are watching a film, your heart, lungs and blood circulation are all reacting to your activity.

Fun facts

Blood squirter
The human heart can create enough pressure to squirt blood at a distance of about 9 metres (30 feet).

Faster breathers
Children and women breathe at a faster rate than men.

The giraffe has a longer neck than you – and bigger lungs! Its lungs are about nine times the size of a human's.

Full of air
A giraffe's lungs can hold 55 litres (12 gallons) of air, while the average human can hold only 6 litres (1.3 gallons).

Floating organs
Your lungs are the only organs in your body that can float on water.

Big breather
Manjit Singh from Leicestershire holds the record for the world's most powerful lungs. He used his lung power to inflate a balloon to a diameter of nearly 2.5 metres (over 8 feet) in 42 minutes.

Every breath you take
On average, a person breathes about 20,000 times a day.

Every beat you make
The human heart beats more than 30 million times a year.

Big-hearted
A human heart weighs between 250 and 300 grams (9-10 ounces), but the heart of a blue whale can weigh over 900 kilograms (1,980 lbs) – that's the same as the weight of a small car!

Blue-blooded
Octopuses have three hearts and blue blood.

Bloody defence
Some lizards can squirt blood from their eyes as a defence mechanism. They shoot the blood into their attackers' mouths, and the taste of it seems to send predators packing.

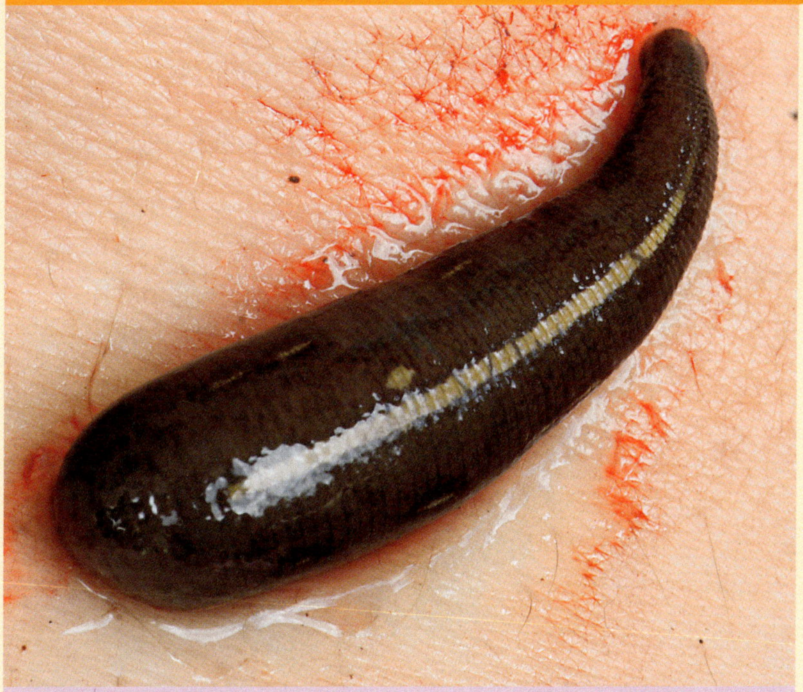

Leeches are still used in medicine today. They can suck away excess blood from an area and help restore a healthy blood supply to damaged tissue.

Delicate veins

The wings of a butterfly contain an intricate system of veins that circulate blood.

Cool ears!

Elephants have lots of blood vessels in their ears. On a hot day, they flap their ears to cool the blood inside. This blood then circulates through the rest of the body, helping the elephant to cool down.

Blood suckers

Leeches have three jaws which are able to break the skin of animals and humans, in order to suck their blood. They can consume 10 times their own body weight in blood. Leeches have been used in medicine for over 2,000 years, and are still used today around the world.

Don't lose it!

You can lose one third of your blood and survive, but if you lose half your blood, you won't.

Long and winding road

Your blood travels through about 100,000 kilometres (62,500 miles) of blood vessels several times every day. Your blood vessels would stretch more than twice around the world if joined end to end.

Thicker than water

Blood is approximately three times thicker than water.

Bags of blood!

The world's biggest blood donation drive took place in India in 2004. A staggering 17,921 people donated blood.

Number crunching

On average, people have at least 5 litres (8.8 pints) of blood in their bodies containing approximately 333,200 million blood cells.

Barrels of blood

In an average lifetime, the human heart pumps about one million barrels of blood.

Activities

Questions

1 Which of these types of exercise is aerobic and which is anaerobic?

Swimming, jogging, weightlifting

2 Does the brain alter the breathing rate (frequency of inhaling and exhaling) in response to the level of oxygen or carbon dioxide in the blood?

3 Do doctors use blood-sucking leeches in some operations on humans?

4 How many red blood cells are in a drop of blood the size of a pinhead?

a) 250 b) 2,500 c) 250,000 d) 250 million

5 How much of our blood is made up of water?

a) 20 per cent b) 50 per cent c) 80 per cent

6 What is the name for the wall of muscle that separates the two sides of the heart?

7 Artificial blood can be used instead of real blood. True or false?

Swimming is a good workout for the heart and lungs.

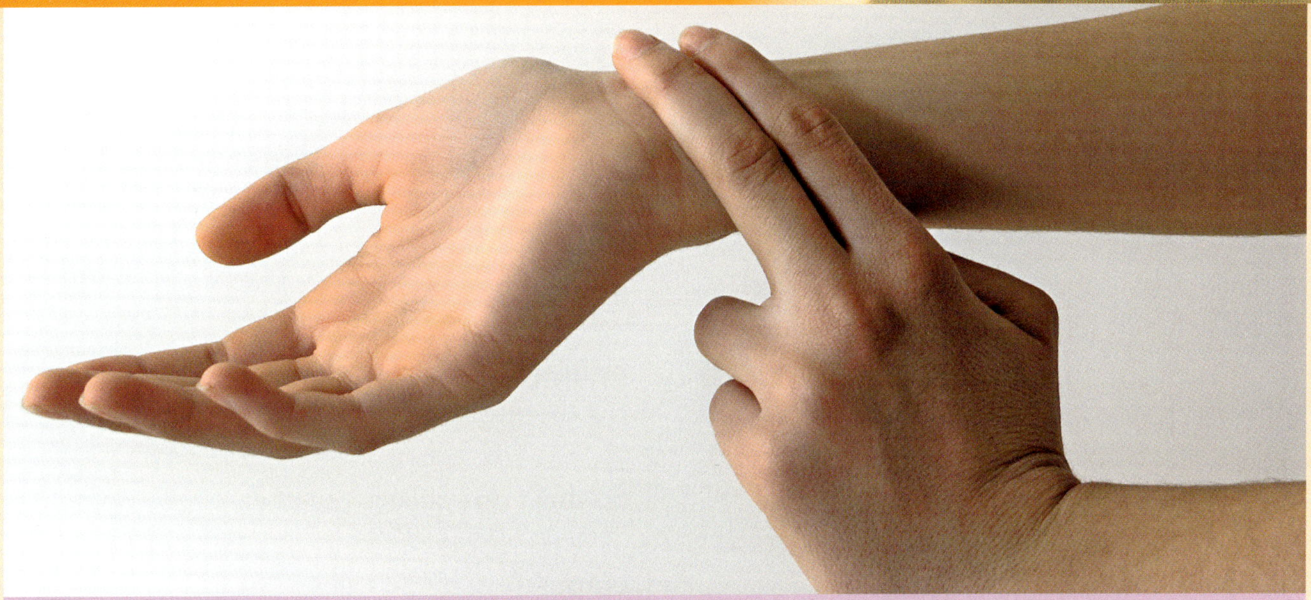

Taking your pulse tells you how many times your heart beats in one minute. It can be felt in places where an artery passes under the skin, such as the wrist, neck and top of the foot.

Take your pulse

Hold one hand out, palm facing up and elbow straight. Press lightly with the index and middle fingers of the other hand on the underside of the wrist, just under the thumb bone.

Count the number of beats you can feel in one minute (look at a clock with a second hand). A normal resting heart rate for an adult is about 60-90 beats per minute. Take your pulse again after 5 minutes of vigorous exercise. If you are fit, you should aim to keep your pulse rate at over 150 beats per minute for 15 minutes of exercise.

Check your breathing

How many breaths do you take each minute? (One breath is an inhalation and an exhalation.) Watch a clock and count how many breaths you take in one minute. Note the number on a piece of paper. Repeat the exercise two more times. Find the average by adding up the amounts and dividing by three.

Next, marching on the spot count the number of breaths you take in one minute. Repeat this two times, and find the average number of breaths. What is the effect of exercise on your respiration rate?

Answers

1 Swimming and jogging are aerobic; weightlifting is anaerobic

2 Carbon dioxide

3 Some doctors use blood-sucking leeches to prevent blood clots in a blood vessel during an operation. The leech sucks blood and releases natural chemicals which prevent the blood from clotting.

4 d) 250 million

5 c) 80 per cent

6 The septum

7 False. Artificial blood can be used to carry out some of the blood's functions, but not all of them – blood cannot be replaced by anything else.

Glossary

alveoli thin-walled bags in the lungs through which oxygen passes into the capillaries

anaemia a lack of certain substances in the blood, including haemoglobin

antibody a substance produced by some white blood cells to fight germs

artery a blood vessel that carries blood from the heart

atrium a top chamber of the heart (plural: atria)

bacteria a type of germ; some bacteria are healthy and others cause disease

bile liquid produced by the liver that contains waste products and helps the body to digest fats

blood pressure the force of blood pushing against the walls of the arteries

blood vessels arteries, veins and capillaries that carry blood

bronchi branches from the lungs along which air travels (singular: bronchus)

capillary a thin-walled blood vessel that delivers oxygen and nutrients to the body's cells

carbohydrate one of the main nutrients in food

cardiovascular system the action of the heart and blood in pumping blood around the body

cell a tiny unit of living matter in the body

cholesterol a substance in the body and also present in some foods

circulatory system the flow and function of the blood

contract to squeeze together

corpuscle a blood cell

digestive system the action of organs that break down food substances and carry waste out of the body

external respiration breathing

faeces solid waste matter from the stomach and digestive system

gene chemical instruction contained in DNA which determines how an individual's cells grow and function

glucose a sugar found in food, it is broken down in the blood for use as energy

haemoglobin an oxygen-carrying protein found in red blood cells

immune system the body's natural defence against infection

internal respiration a chemical reaction in the cells

lymph nodes body parts containing white blood cells for fighting infection

minerals natural chemicals that are found in food and used by the body

nervous system the action of the brain, spinal cord and network of nerves

plasma the yellow liquid in the blood which transports blood cells

platelets tiny fragments of cells in the blood that clump together to form a clot

protein a substance produced in the cells; a substance found in some foods

respiratory system the action of the lungs and airways in delivering oxygen into, and expelling carbon dioxide from, the body

septum the muscle that separates the left and right sides of the heart

spleen an organ that breaks down old blood cells and helps fight infection

tissue a group of similar cells

urine liquid waste produced by the kidneys

vein a blood vessel that carries blood towards the heart

ventricle a bottom chamber of the heart

virus a type of germ that causes illness

Further information

Body Science: The Heart in Action,
Richard Walker,
Watts, 2006

Our Bodies: Heart, Lungs and Blood,
Steve Parker,
Wayland, 2007

What happens when your heart beats?
Jacqui Bailey,
Wayland, 2007

Websites

http://health.howstuffworks.com/body-systems-channel.htm
Follow the links to find out about the circulatory and respiratory systems.

http://www.smm.org/heart/heart/top.html
This website contains animations, interactive tasks and amazing facts about the heart and lungs.

http://www.fi.edu/learn/heart/index.html
Get information about the circulatory and respiratory systems from the Franklin Institute.

http://www.kidskonnect.com/content/view/337/27
This website contains facts and detailed information about the cardiovascular and respiratory systems.

Index